Sunset

Light
Desserts

By the Editors of Sunset Books
and Sunset Magazine

Lane Publishing Co. • Menlo Park, California

Research & Text
Claire Coleman

Coordinating Editor
Linda J. Selden

Design
Cynthia Hanson

Illustrations
Chad Kubo

Photography
Victor Budnik

Food Stylist
Karen Hazarian

Treat Yourself!

Torn between virtue and indulgence? Now you can enjoy both, with this irresistible collection of light desserts. Each one is a luscious and satisfying treat that will taste like a splurge with every bite, and yet each meets today's preference for eating fresh, healthful foods that are low in fat and calories.

Our light desserts don't seem like "diet food" because they're not. They simply take advantage of the goodness of naturally light ingredients; only the excess calories are gone. From moist and tender cakes to fluffy soufflés, from elegant fruit desserts to creamy frozen creations, you'll find ideas here to satisfy every craving—even chocolate. Best of all, you don't have to feel guilty—so save room for dessert!

For our recipes, we provide a nutritional analysis prepared by Hill Nutrition Associates, Inc., of New York, stating calorie count; grams of protein, carbohydrate, and total fat; and milligrams of cholesterol and sodium. Generally, the nutritional information applies to a single serving, based on the largest number of servings given for each recipe.

The nutritional analysis does not include optional ingredients or those for which no specific amount is stated. If an ingredient is listed with an option, the information was calculated using the first choice. Likewise, if a range is given for the amount of an ingredient, values were figured based on the first, lower amount.

We extend special thanks to Rebecca La Brum for carefully editing the manuscript; to Kathleen Volkmann, Caroline Cory, Scott Gill, Annie Glass Studio, Britex Fabrics, and Dianne McKenzie for their assistance with our photography; and to Jacqueline Osborn for her help with the graphics.

Cover: Guaranteed to add excitement to your dinner menu, without a lot of extra calories, is Frozen Tarragon Mousse with Strawberries (page 74). The tarragon is an unexpectedly appealing addition to the mousse; its aromatic sweetness makes a fine complement to the flavor of the berries. Photography by Victor Budnik. Food styling by Karen Hazarian.

Sunset Books
  Editor: David E. Clark
  Managing Editor: Elizabeth L. Hogan

First printing May 1987

CONTENTS

For a dessert that's light, elegant, and full
of natural fruit flavor, offer
Pear Fan with Orange Syrup (page 45).

Special Features

Cakes, Pies, Cookies & Crêpes

TRADITIONAL BAKED TREATS

Cakes, pies, cookies, and crêpes are often considered the most sinful of desserts, but this need not be so. By choosing recipes low in fat, you can enjoy a variety of baked goodies with a clear conscience. There are plenty of choices—delicately sweet Angel Food Cake, cinnamon-scented yogurt-filled Spiced Pumpkin Roll, tangy Lime Angel Pie, and many more.

How is it possible? Our Ricotta Cheesecake is made with lowfat ricotta cheese instead of cream cheese. Lime Angel Pie uses a fluffy meringue shell instead of rich pie pastry. Many other recipes feature chiffon fillings and fruit toppings instead of heavier creams and frostings. If you use light ingredients, it's easy to make great-tasting baked goods that won't weigh you down.

Orange Chiffon Cake

Preparation time: 20 to 25 minutes
Baking time: about 1 hour and 10 minutes

Calories per serving: 242

Standing tall on your cake plate, a chiffon cake makes an attractive dessert to slice and serve at the table. This one is orange-flavored; beaten egg whites give it a springy texture.

2¼ cups **cake flour**
1½ cups **sugar**
1 tablespoon **baking powder**
¾ teaspoon **salt**
½ cup **salad oil**
6 **egg yolks**
¾ cup **orange juice**
2 tablespoons **grated orange peel**
1 cup (about 8) **egg whites**
½ teaspoon **cream of tartar**
3½ to 4 cups **strawberries,** hulled, sliced, and sweetened to taste; or **Strawberry Sauce** (recipe follows)

In a large bowl, stir together flour, 1 cup of the sugar, baking powder, and salt. Make a well in center of flour mixture and add oil, egg yolks, orange juice, and orange peel; mix well.

In large bowl of an electric mixer, beat egg whites with cream of tartar until they hold soft peaks. Gradually add remaining ½ cup sugar and continue to beat until mixture holds stiff peaks. Gently fold egg yolk mixture into beaten whites; pour batter into an ungreased 10-inch tube pan with a removable bottom.

Bake in a 325° oven until top of cake is browned (about 1 hour and 10 minutes). Invert pan on a funnel or soda pop bottle (this prevents cake from shrinking and falling) and let cake cool completely; then remove from pan.

To serve, cut cake into slices; top each slice with sweetened strawberries or Strawberry Sauce. Makes 14 to 16 servings.

Strawberry Sauce. In a 2- to 3-quart pan, stir together ½ cup **sugar,** 1½ tablespoons **cornstarch,** 1 cup **orange juice,** and ¼ cup **orange-flavored liqueur** (or additional orange juice) until smooth. Bring to a boil over medium-high heat, stirring until clear and thickened. Stir in 6 cups sliced hulled **strawberries** until well combined. Let cool.

Per serving: 4 grams protein, 36 grams carbohydrates, 9 grams total fat, 102 milligrams cholesterol, 212 milligrams sodium.

German Fruit Kuchen

Preparation time: 40 to 50 minutes
Baking time: 18 to 20 minutes

Calories per serving: 244

This unusual cake (called *Obstkuchen* in German) has a recessed center to fill with a topping of cherries or other fresh summer fruit. The lemon-scented cake is baked in a special pan, sometimes called a Mary Ann or flan pan and often sold in cookware shops. If you can't find one, use a standard tart pan.

2 **eggs**
½ cup **sugar**
¼ teaspoon **grated lemon peel**
2 tablespoons **water**
¾ cup **all-purpose flour**
1 teaspoon **baking powder**
Cherry Topping (recipe follows); or 4 to 5 cups **berries** or sliced **peaches,** sweetened to taste

In large bowl of an electric mixer, combine eggs, sugar, and lemon peel. Beat on high speed until thick, creamy, and pale in color (6 to 10 minutes). Add water; continue to beat until foamy (about 2 more minutes). Mix flour and baking powder; add to egg mixture and beat on medium speed until well blended.

Spoon batter into a well-greased 10- or 11-inch flan or tart pan with a base that forms a well when pan is inverted (or use a standard tart pan). Bake in a 325° oven until top of cake springs back when lightly pressed (18 to 20 minutes). Let cool in pan on a rack for 10 minutes, then turn out of pan onto a serving plate.

Prepare Cherry Topping; spoon into center of cake. Makes 8 servings.

Cherry Topping. Stem and pit 7 to 8 cups **sweet cherries.** In a 2- to 3-quart pan, combine 3 cups of the cherries with ⅓ cup **water.** Bring to a full boil over medium heat, crushing fruit with a potato masher. Pour into a fine wire strainer set over a bowl and press to extract juice; you should have about 1¼ cups juice. Discard pulp.

In pan used to cook cherries, blend 1 tablespoon **cornstarch** and ¼ cup **sugar.** Gradually mix in cherry juice, stirring until smooth. Then stir over medium-high heat until sauce boils and thickens. Stir in 2 tablespoons **lemon juice.** Let cool, then stir in remaining whole pitted cherries.

Per serving: 4 grams protein, 53 grams carbohydrates, 3 grams total fat, 69 milligrams cholesterol, 72 milligrams sodium.

Ground nuts and sherry wine add appealing flavor and texture to Sherry Sponge Cake (recipe on facing page). Serve it plain, or adorn it with a snowy dusting of powdered sugar or an orange slice and a few thin shreds of orange peel.

· ·

Chocolate-glazed Génoise

Preparation time: 40 to 50 minutes
Baking time: 35 to 45 minutes

Calories per serving: 223

Standard in the repertoire of French pastry chefs, *génoise*—thought to have originated in the Italian city of Genoa—is a buttery sponge cake made in one bowl. This versatile cake is a component of many sumptuous desserts; those who want to eat light can enjoy it with a simple chocolate glaze or flavorful fruit sauce instead of the usual rich buttercream.

   3 **eggs**
   ½ **cup sugar**
   ½ **cup sifted cake flour**
   ½ **teaspoon vanilla**
   3 **tablespoons butter or margarine, melted and cooled**
      Chocolate Glaze (recipe follows) or Raspberry Sauce (page 40)

Place eggs and sugar in large bowl of an electric mixer; stir just until combined. Set bowl over a pan containing about 2 inches of simmering water (water should not boil or touch bowl). Let stand, stirring occasionally, until mixture is just warm to the touch. Remove bowl from over water. Beat egg mixture on high speed until thick, foamy, pale in color, and about tripled in volume (8 to 10 minutes).

Sprinkle flour, about 2 tablespoons at a time, over egg mixture; fold in each addition gently but thoroughly. Swirl vanilla into butter. Drizzle butter mixture over top of batter; fold in gently but thoroughly. Pour batter into a greased, flour-dusted 9-inch spring-form pan or 9-inch round cake pan with a removable bottom.

Bake in a 325° oven until cake is lightly browned and begins to pull away from pan edges (35 to 45 minutes). Loosen edges of cake with a spatula; remove pan sides immediately, transfer cake to a rack, and let cool completely.

Prepare Chocolate Glaze; spread over top and sides of cake. (Or leave cake plain and offer Raspberry Sauce to top individual servings.) Makes 8 servings.

Chocolate Glaze. In the top of a double boiler, combine 4 ounces **semisweet chocolate** and 1 tablespoon **butter** or margarine. Stir over barely simmering water just until melted. Remove from heat and let cool, stirring occasionally, until slightly thickened.

Per serving: 3 grams protein, 26 grams carbohydrates, 13 grams total fat, 118 milligrams cholesterol, 85 milligrams sodium.

Sherry Sponge Cake

(Pictured on facing page)
Preparation time: 30 to 40 minutes
Baking time: about 1 hour

Calories per serving: 254

Looking for a special dessert? Choose this firm-textured, wine-flavored sponge cake, fragrant with cinnamon and almonds. Lightly dusted with powdered sugar and garnished with oranges, it's a perfect partner for coffee, tea, or dessert wine.

   ¾ **cup whole blanched or unblanched almonds**
   1¼ **cups all-purpose flour**
   ¼ **teaspoon salt**
   ½ **teaspoon ground cinnamon**
   8 **eggs, separated**
   1½ **cups granulated sugar**
   ⅓ **cup *each* sweet sherry and orange juice**
      Powdered sugar (optional)
      Orange slices and shredded orange peel (optional)

In a food processor or blender, whirl almonds until finely ground.

Sift flour, salt, and cinnamon into a large bowl; stir in ground almonds until well mixed, then set mixture aside.

In large bowl of an electric mixer, beat egg whites until they hold stiff, moist peaks. Set aside. In another bowl, beat egg yolks on high speed until thick and lemon-colored; gradually add granulated sugar and continue to beat, scraping bowl often, until mixture is creamy and pale in color. Stir in sherry and orange juice. Fold flour mixture into yolk mixture; then fold in beaten egg whites gently but thoroughly.

Pour batter into an ungreased 9- or 10-inch tube pan with a removable bottom. Bake in a 325° oven until top of cake springs back when lightly pressed (about 1 hour). Invert pan on a funnel or soda pop bottle (this prevents cake from shrinking and falling) and let cake cool completely; then carefully remove from pan.

To serve, sift powdered sugar lightly over cake, if desired; then cut into slices. Garnish each serving with orange slices and orange peel, if you wish. Makes about 12 servings.

Per serving: 7 grams protein, 38 grams carbohydrates, 8 grams total fat, 183 milligrams cholesterol, 93 milligrams sodium.

Yellow Sponge Cake Roll

Preparation time: 60 to 70 minutes
Baking time: about 12 minutes

Calories per serving: 220

Leavened by beaten egg whites, sponge cakes are characteristically light and fluffy. This one is golden and delicate, with a velvety texture and a slightly sweet flavor. Spread it with your favorite jam, then roll up and dust with powdered sugar for a dessert that's pretty, festive, and ethereally light.

- **4 eggs, separated**
- **¾ cup granulated sugar**
- **1 teaspoon vanilla**
- **¾ cup sifted cake flour**
- **¾ teaspoon baking powder**
- **¼ teaspoon salt**
- **⅓ cup powdered sugar**
- **1 cup jam, warmed**

Lightly grease a rimmed 10- by 15-inch baking pan and line it with wax paper; grease paper and set pan aside.

In large bowl of an electric mixer, beat egg yolks on high speed until thick and lemon-colored. Gradually add ½ cup of the granulated sugar and continue to beat, scraping bowl often, until mixture is creamy and pale in color. Stir in vanilla. Stir together flour, baking powder, and salt. Sprinkle flour mixture over egg yolk mixture, about ¼ cup at a time, folding in each addition gently but thoroughly.

In another bowl, beat egg whites until they hold soft peaks. Gradually add remaining ¼ cup granulated sugar, 1 tablespoon at a time, and continue to beat until mixture holds stiff, glossy peaks. Fold in yolk mixture just until blended. Pour batter into prepared pan and spread evenly.

Bake in a 375° oven until top of cake springs back when lightly pressed (about 12 minutes). Immediately invert cake onto a dishtowel sprinkled with 3 tablespoons of the powdered sugar. Peel off wax paper; immediately roll cake and towel into a cylinder, starting with a short edge. Let cool completely on a rack.

Unroll cake and spread with jam, then reroll. If made ahead, wrap filled cake in plastic wrap and refrigerate for up to 24 hours. Sift remaining powdered sugar over top of cake before serving. Makes 10 servings.

Per serving: 3 grams protein, 47 grams carbohydrates, 2 grams total fat, 110 milligrams cholesterol, 118 milligrams sodium.

Apple Sponge Roll

Preparation time: about 1½ hours
Baking time: about 15 minutes
Chilling time: at least 2 hours

Calories per serving: 209

Apples, nuts, and raisins simmer together to make the juicy fruit filling for this delicate sponge cake lightly accented with lemon.

- **Apple Filling (recipe follows)**
- **5 eggs, separated**
- **1 cup granulated sugar**
- **¾ teaspoon grated lemon peel**
- **1 tablespoon lemon juice**
- **¾ cup all-purpose flour**
- **⅓ cup powdered sugar**

Prepare Apple Filling and refrigerate.

Lightly grease a rimmed 10- by 15-inch baking pan and line it with wax paper; grease paper and set pan aside.

In large bowl of an electric mixer, beat egg whites until foamy; gradually add ½ cup of the granulated sugar and continue to beat until mixture holds stiff, glossy peaks. Set aside. In another bowl, beat egg yolks on high speed until thick and lemon-colored. Gradually add remaining ½ cup granulated sugar and continue to beat, scraping bowl often, until mixture is creamy and pale in color. Gently stir in lemon peel and lemon juice. Sprinkle in flour, about ¼ cup at a time, gently folding in each addition. Fold in egg white mixture. Pour batter into prepared pan and spread evenly.

Bake in a 375° oven until top of cake springs back when lightly pressed (about 15 minutes). Immediately invert cake onto a dishtowel sprinkled with 3 tablespoons of the powdered sugar. Peel off wax paper; immediately roll cake and towel into a cylinder, starting with a long edge. Let cool completely on a rack.

Unroll cake and spread with filling, then reroll. Wrap filled cake in plastic wrap and refrigerate for at least 2 hours or up to 24 hours. Sift remaining powdered sugar over top of cake before serving. Makes 14 servings.

Apple Filling. In a 2- to 3-quart pan, combine 4 cups peeled, chopped **apples;** ½ cup *each* **apple jelly, raisins,** and chopped **almonds;** and 2 tablespoons **lemon juice.** Cook, uncovered, over medium heat until apples are tender to bite; stir often. Let cool, then cover and refrigerate until well chilled.

Per serving: 4 grams protein, 40 grams carbohydrates, 5 grams total fat, 98 milligrams cholesterol, 29 milligrams sodium.

Chocolate Sponge Cake

Preparation time: 25 to 30 minutes
Baking time: 25 to 30 minutes

Calories per serving: 146

A chocolate dessert that's light and lowfat? Here it is—a feathery sponge cake flavored with cocoa. It has its origins in the classic French *génoise*, but there's not a bit of butter added. Dust the cake with powdered sugar for a pastry-shop finish.

⅔ **cup sifted cake flour**
¼ **cup sifted unsweetened cocoa**
3 **eggs**
¾ **cup granulated sugar**
¼ **teaspoon *each* salt and vanilla**
3 **tablespoons water**
2 **tablespoons powdered sugar**

Lightly grease a 9-inch round baking pan and line bottom with wax paper; grease paper and set pan aside. Stir together flour and cocoa; set aside.

In large bowl of an electric mixer, beat eggs on high speed until thick and lemon-colored. Gradually add granulated sugar and continue to beat, scraping bowl often, until mixture is creamy and pale in color. Beat in salt, vanilla, and water.

Sprinkle flour mixture over egg mixture, about ⅓ cup at a time, gently folding in each addition. Pour into prepared pan; spread evenly.

Bake in a 375° oven until top of cake springs back when lightly pressed (25 to 30 minutes). Let cool in pan on a rack for 5 minutes, then turn out onto rack and let cool completely. Sift powdered sugar over top of cake before serving. Makes 8 servings.

Per serving: 3 grams protein, 29 grams carbohydrates, 3 grams total fat, 103 milligrams cholesterol, 94 milligrams sodium.

Blackberry-Lemon Cake Roll

Preparation time: 50 to 60 minutes
Baking time: about 15 minutes
Chilling time: at least 2 hours

Calories per serving: 205

Tender sponge cake swirls around sweet, plump berries and a creamy lemon filling for this special-occasion dessert. Though the recipe calls for black-berries, you could just as well use boysenberries, loganberries, or olallieberries in their place.

4 **eggs, separated**
¾ **cup granulated sugar**
⅔ **cup all-purpose flour**
1 **teaspoon baking powder**
¼ **teaspoon salt**
⅓ **cup powdered sugar**
  Lemon Filling (recipe follows)
5 **to 6 cups blackberries**
  Granulated sugar

Lightly grease a rimmed 10- by 15-inch baking pan and line it with wax paper; grease paper and set pan aside.

In large bowl of an electric mixer, beat egg yolks and ½ cup of the granulated sugar on high speed until thick and lemon-colored. Blend flour with baking powder; fold into yolk mixture gently but thoroughly.

In another bowl, combine egg whites and salt; beat until foamy. Gradually add ¼ cup granulated sugar and continue to beat until mixture holds stiff, moist peaks; fold into yolk mixture. Pour batter into prepared pan and spread evenly.

Bake in a 375° oven until top of cake springs back when lightly pressed (about 15 minutes). Immediately invert cake onto a dishtowel sprinkled with 3 tablespoons of the powdered sugar. Peel off wax paper; immediately roll cake and towel into a cylinder, starting with a long edge. Let cool completely on a rack.

Prepare Lemon Filling while cake is cooling. Unroll cooled cake and spread with filling; sprinkle evenly with 1½ cups of the blackberries. Reroll, wrap in plastic wrap, and refrigerate for at least 2 hours or up to 6 hours.

To serve, sift remaining powdered sugar over top of cake. Sweeten remaining 3½ to 4½ cups black-berries to taste with granulated sugar; offer sweetened blackberries to spoon over slices of cake. Makes 14 servings.

Lemon Filling. In a small pan, blend 1 tablespoon **cornstarch** and ½ cup **sugar.** Stir in ⅓ cup **lemon juice,** 1 teaspoon grated **lemon peel,** and 3 table-spoons **water.** Bring to a boil over medium heat; cook, stirring, until clear and thickened. In a small bowl, lightly beat 1 **egg;** stir in about 2 tablespoons of the hot lemon mixture, then stir egg mixture back into pan. Reduce heat to low and cook, stirring, for 1 minute. Add 2 tablespoons **butter** or margarine and stir until melted; let cool to room temperature.

In a small bowl, beat ½ cup **whipping cream** until it holds soft peaks. Fold into cooled lemon mixture.

Per serving: 3 grams protein, 34 grams carbohydrates, 7 grams total fat, 112 milligrams cholesterol, 115 milligrams sodium.

Mocha Roll

Preparation time: 60 to 70 minutes
Baking time: about 12 minutes
Chilling time: at least 4 hours

Calories per serving: 173

Chocolate and cinnamon flavor this moist and delicate cake roll; the creamy filling is accented with coffee.

> ¾ **cup sifted all-purpose flour**
> ¼ **cup sifted unsweetened cocoa**
> 1 **teaspoon baking powder**
> ¼ **teaspoon salt**
> ½ **teaspoon ground cinnamon**
> 3 **eggs**
> ½ **cup** *each* **firmly packed light brown sugar and granulated sugar**
> ⅓ **cup water**
> 1 **teaspoon vanilla**
> ⅓ **cup powdered sugar**
> **Creamy Coffee Filling (recipe follows)**

Lightly grease a rimmed 10- by 15-inch baking pan and line it with wax paper; grease paper and set pan aside. Stir together flour, cocoa, baking powder, salt, and cinnamon; set aside.

In large bowl of an electric mixer, beat eggs on high speed until thick and lemon-colored. Force brown sugar through a strainer to get rid of any hard lumps. Gradually add brown sugar and granulated sugar to eggs; continue to beat, scraping bowl often, until mixture is creamy and pale in color. With a rubber spatula, mix in water and vanilla.

Sprinkle flour mixture over egg mixture, about ⅓ cup at a time; gently fold in each addition. Pour batter into prepared pan and spread evenly.

Bake in a 375° oven until top of cake springs back when lightly pressed (about 12 minutes). Immediately invert cake onto a dishtowel sprinkled with 3 tablespoons of the powdered sugar. Peel off wax paper and immediately roll cake and towel into a cylinder, starting with a long edge. Let cool completely on a rack.

Prepare Creamy Coffee Filling. Unroll cake and spread with filling, then reroll. Wrap in plastic wrap and refrigerate for at least 4 or up to 24 hours. Sift remaining powdered sugar over cake before serving. Makes 14 servings.

Creamy Coffee Filling. In small bowl of an electric mixer, beat 1 cup **whipping cream** with 3 tablespoons **sugar** until mixture holds soft peaks. Add ½ teaspoon **ground cinnamon** and ¾ teaspoon **instant coffee;** beat until mixture holds stiff peaks.

Per serving: 3 grams protein, 27 grams carbohydrates, 7 grams total fat, 78 milligrams cholesterol, 92 milligrams sodium.

Spiced Pumpkin Roll

(Pictured on facing page)
Preparation time: 50 to 60 minutes
Baking time: about 15 minutes
Freezing time: 2 to 3 hours

Calories per serving: 190

This frozen cake roll boasts the flavors of pumpkin pie à la mode, but it has a fancier appearance and only a fraction of the calories. It's a festive offering after any meal—and a perfect finish for a holiday feast.

> ¾ **cup all-purpose flour**
> 2 **teaspoons ground cinnamon**
> 1 **teaspoon** *each* **baking powder and ground ginger**
> ½ **teaspoon** *each* **ground nutmeg and salt**
> 3 **eggs**
> 1 **cup granulated sugar**
> ⅔ **cup canned solid-pack pumpkin**
> ⅓ **cup powdered sugar**
> 1 **quart Vanilla Frozen Yogurt (page 72) or purchased frozen yogurt, slightly softened**
> **Shredded orange peel (optional)**

Grease a rimmed 10- by 15-inch baking pan and line it with wax paper; grease paper and set pan aside.

In a small bowl, stir together flour, cinnamon, baking powder, ginger, nutmeg, and salt; set aside. In large bowl of an electric mixer, beat eggs on high speed until thick and lemon-colored. Gradually add granulated sugar and continue to beat, scraping bowl often, until mixture is creamy and pale in color. With mixer on low speed, mix in pumpkin and flour mixture. Pour batter into prepared pan and spread evenly.

Bake in a 375° oven until top of cake springs back when lightly pressed (about 15 minutes). Immediately invert onto a dishtowel sprinkled with 3 tablespoons of the powdered sugar. Peel off wax paper and immediately roll cake and towel into a cylinder, starting with a long edge. Let cool completely on a rack.

Unroll cake, spread with yogurt, and reroll. Wrap in plastic wrap and freeze until firm (2 to 3 hours). To serve, unwrap cake roll and place on a serving plate. Let stand at room temperature for 10 to 15 minutes, then sift remaining powdered sugar over top. Cut cake into slices; garnish each slice with a little orange peel, if desired. Makes 14 servings.

Per serving: 5 grams protein, 36 grams carbohydrates, 3 grams total fat, 93 milligrams cholesterol, 163 milligrams sodium.

When the weather's brisk and the leaves begin to turn, a welcome dessert is
Spiced Pumpkin Roll (recipe on facing page). Made with moist pumpkin cake and
Vanilla Frozen Yogurt (recipe on page 72), it tastes much like pumpkin pie à la mode.

· ·

Angel Food Cake

Preparation time: 20 to 30 minutes
Baking time: 30 to 35 minutes

Calories per serving: 127

Snowy white and temptingly tender, angel food cake has long been a favorite light dessert. If desired, you can give it a fancier appearance by sifting powdered sugar over the top before serving.

> 1 **cup sifted cake flour**
> 1¼ **cups granulated sugar**
> 1½ **cups (about 12) egg whites**
> ½ **teaspoon salt**
> 2 **teaspoons cream of tartar**
> 1½ **teaspoons vanilla or almond extract**
>   **Powdered sugar (optional)**

Sift together flour and ½ cup of the granulated sugar; sift again and set aside. In large bowl of an electric mixer, beat egg whites until foamy. Add salt and cream of tartar and continue to beat until mixture holds soft peaks. Add remaining ¾ cup granulated sugar, 2 tablespoons at a time, beating well after each addition; continue to beat until mixture holds stiff peaks.

With a rubber spatula, fold in vanilla. Then sprinkle in flour mixture, about ¼ cup at a time, gently folding in each addition just until blended. Pour batter into an ungreased 10-inch tube pan with a removable bottom and gently smooth top. Slide rubber spatula into batter and run it around pan to eliminate large air bubbles.

Bake in a 375° oven until top of cake is golden and springs back when lightly pressed (30 to 35 minutes). Invert pan on a funnel or soda pop bottle (this prevents cake from shrinking and falling) and let cake cool completely; then remove from pan. If desired, lightly sift powdered sugar over top of cake. Makes about 12 servings.

Per serving: 4 grams protein, 28 grams carbohydrates, .06 gram total fat, 0 milligram cholesterol, 142 milligrams sodium.

Cherry Savarin Cake

Preparation time: 50 to 60 minutes
Baking time: about 35 minutes

Calories per serving: 241

Baked in a ring mold and crowned with cherry preserves, this syrup-soaked cake presents a pretty picture. (Before beating the eggs, bring them to room temperature; they'll increase in volume more quickly.)

>   **Lemon Syrup (recipe follows)**
> 6 **eggs**
> 1 **tablespoon lemon juice**
> ¼ **teaspoon salt**
> 1 **cup sugar**
> 1 **cup all-purpose flour**
> ¾ **cup cherry preserves**

Prepare Lemon Syrup and set aside.

In large bowl of an electric mixer, beat eggs, lemon juice, and salt on high speed until thick, lemon-colored, and several times greater in volume (10 to 15 minutes). Turn mixer speed to medium and add sugar, 1 tablespoon at a time; continue to beat, scraping bowl often, until mixture is creamy and pale in color. Then sprinkle in flour, about ¼ cup at a time, folding in each addition just until blended.

Spoon batter into a greased, flour-dusted 3-quart ring mold. Bake in a 325° oven until a wooden pick inserted in center of cake comes out clean (about 35 minutes). Immediately poke a wooden skewer all the way through cake at 1-inch intervals. Spoon half the cooled Lemon Syrup over hot cake; let stand for 15 minutes. Loosen cake from pan and invert onto a serving plate. Spoon remaining syrup over cake, letting it soak in.

In a small pan, heat preserves just until melted; spoon evenly over cake. Let cool before serving. Makes 12 servings.

Lemon Syrup. In a small pan, combine ⅓ cup **lemon juice**, 2 strips **lemon peel** (*each* about ½ by 2 inches, yellow part only), and ⅔ cup *each* **sugar** and **water.** Bring to a boil; then reduce heat and simmer, uncovered, stirring constantly, until sugar is dissolved. Let cool; remove lemon peel.

Per serving: 4 grams protein, 50 grams carbohydrates, 3 grams total fat, 137 milligrams cholesterol, 84 milligrams sodium.

Crêpes Suzette

Preparation time: 50 to 60 minutes
Cooking time: 30 to 40 minutes

Calories per serving: 201

Once considered the very epitome of an elegant French dessert, crêpes Suzette have been pushed from the spotlight by more recent culinary creations. But we think these delicate pancakes, bathed in citrus syrup and set dramatically aflame, still have a lot to recommend them. For an especially showy presentation, you can make the crêpes right at the table in a chafing dish.

16 **Basic Crêpes** (recipe follows)
¼ **cup butter or margarine**
6 **tablespoons sugar**
1½ **teaspoons grated orange peel**
½ **teaspoon grated lemon peel**
⅓ **cup orange juice**
2 **teaspoons lemon juice**
¼ **cup orange-flavored liqueur**
Orange slices (optional)

Prepare Basic Crêpes; fold each in half.

Melt butter in a wide frying pan over medium-high heat. Add sugar; cook, stirring, until bubbling vigorously (do not allow butter to brown).

Add orange peel, lemon peel, orange juice, and lemon juice. Bring to a full boil. Add folded crêpes, 1 at a time; as each is moistened, fold in half again to make a triangle and push to side of pan.

When all crêpes are heated, arrange evenly in pan. Warm liqueur in a small pan (do not bring to a boil). Carefully ignite with a match (not beneath an exhaust fan or near flammable items); pour over crêpes and shake pan until flame dies down. Let simmer for a few minutes, then spoon crêpes and sauce onto serving plates. Garnish each serving with orange slices, if desired. Makes 5 to 8 servings.

Basic Crêpes. In a blender or food processor, whirl 3 **eggs** and ⅔ cup **all-purpose flour** until blended. With motor running, slowly add 1 cup **lowfat milk;** whirl until smooth.

In a 6- to 7-inch crêpe pan or other flat-bottomed frying pan, melt ¼ teaspoon **butter** or margarine over medium heat; swirl to coat surface. All at once, pour in about 1½ tablespoons of the batter, tilting pan so batter flows quickly over entire flat surface. If heat is correct and pan hot enough, crêpe sets at once and forms tiny bubbles (don't worry if there are a few small holes); if pan is too cool, batter makes a smooth, moist layer. Cook until edges of crêpe are lightly browned and surface feels dry when lightly touched.

To turn, run a wide spatula around edges of crêpe; lay spatula on top of crêpe and very quickly invert pan, flipping crêpe out onto spatula. Then lay crêpe, uncooked surface down, back in pan and cook until lightly browned. Turn crêpe out of pan onto a plate.

Repeat to make each crêpe; stir batter occasionally. Stack crêpes as made. Use within a few hours; or let cool, package airtight, and refrigerate for up to 1 week. To reheat, wrap stacked crêpes in foil and heat in a 350° oven for 10 to 15 minutes. Makes about 16 crêpes.

Per serving: 4 grams protein, 22 grams carbohydrates, 10 grams total fat, 126 milligrams cholesterol, 120 milligrams sodium.

Glazed Peach Crêpes

Preparation time: 1¼ to 1½ hours
Baking time: about 25 minutes

Calories per serving: 222

Accented with nutmeg and lemon, sliced peaches make a warm, fruity filling for these dessert crêpes. As a variation, try sliced apples, nectarines, apricots, or pears in place of the peaches; adjust the amount of sugar to the sweetness of the fruit you're using. You can also make the crêpes with whole wheat flour instead of all-purpose flour; if you do this, be sure to let the batter stand for at least an hour before cooking the crêpes, so the bran has a chance to soften.

8 **Basic Crêpes** (recipe at left)
2 **tablespoons butter or margarine**
6 **medium-size peaches, peeled, pitted, and cut into ½-inch-thick slices; or 6 cups unsweetened frozen peach slices, thawed and patted dry**
1 **teaspoon grated lemon peel**
1 **tablespoon lemon juice**
⅛ **teaspoon ground nutmeg**
⅓ **to ½ cup sugar**
2 **tablespoons brandy**
½ **cup sour cream** (optional)

Prepare Basic Crêpes and set aside.

Melt butter in a wide frying pan over medium heat. Add peaches, lemon peel, lemon juice, and nutmeg. Cook, gently turning peaches occasionally with a wide spatula, until fresh peaches begin to soften (about 7 minutes). Sprinkle in sugar and cook, stirring gently, for 2 more minutes.

Warm brandy in a small pan (do not bring to a boil); carefully ignite with a match (not beneath an exhaust fan or near flammable items), then spoon over peaches. Shake pan until flame dies down; continue to cook until liquid is slightly thickened. Remove from heat and let cool slightly.

To assemble, spoon 3 tablespoons of the peach filling across lower third of each crêpe and roll to enclose. Place filled crêpes, seam side down, in a lightly buttered baking dish. Spoon remaining filling over top.

Cover and bake in a 325° oven until crêpes are heated through (about 25 minutes). If desired, top each serving with 1½ to 2 tablespoons of the sour cream. Makes 4 to 6 servings.

Per serving: 4 grams protein, 38 grams carbohydrates, 7 grams total fat, 84 milligrams cholesterol, 80 milligrams sodium.

Juicy fresh fruit crowns our creamy Ricotta Cheesecake (recipe on facing page).
It's as full of old-fashioned flavor as its traditional
counterparts—all you give up are those unwanted extra calories.

. . . .

Tofu Banana-Pineapple Cheesecake

Preparation time: 30 to 40 minutes
Baking time: about 1 hour
Chilling time: 2 to 3 hours

Calories per serving: 260

Tofu replaces the typical cream cheese in this fruity cheesecake, giving you a dessert that's high in protein, low in cholesterol and calories. Best of all, it's smooth, creamy, and delicious—the tofu's subtle flavor blends well with the sweet bananas and pineapple.

When you shop for ingredients, look for the medium-firm type of tofu. You'll find it packaged in plastic tubs in the fresh produce or the refrigerated section of your market. (Or check an Asian grocery store.)

Graham Cracker Crust (recipe follows)
1 **pound 6 ounces medium-firm tofu (bean curd)**
2 **eggs**
½ **cup firmly packed brown sugar**
2 **tablespoons lemon juice**
1 **teaspoon** *each* **grated lemon peel and vanilla**
2 **medium-size ripe bananas**
1 **can (about 8 oz.) crushed pineapple packed in its own juice, drained**

Prepare Graham Cracker Crust, reserving 1 tablespoon of the crumb mixture as directed; set crust aside.

Drain tofu, pat dry with paper towels, and set aside. In a blender or food processor, combine eggs, sugar, lemon juice, lemon peel, and vanilla. Cut tofu and bananas into chunks; add half the chunks to blender or processor and whirl until smooth. Add remaining tofu and banana chunks and whirl until very smooth. Pour mixture into a bowl and stir in pineapple; then pour into crust.

Bake in a 325° oven until center of cheesecake jiggles only slightly when pan is gently shaken (about 1 hour). Let cool in pan on a rack, then cover and refrigerate until cold (2 to 3 hours).

To serve, remove pan sides and sprinkle cheesecake with reserved crumb mixture. Makes about 8 servings.

Graham Cracker Crust. In a bowl, combine 1 cup **graham cracker crumbs** and 3 tablespoons **butter** or margarine, melted. Reserve 1 tablespoon of the crumb mixture to garnish top of cheesecake; press remaining mixture evenly over bottom of a 9-inch spring-form pan or 9-inch cake pan with a removable bottom. Bake in a 350° oven for 6 minutes; let cool.

Per serving: 9 grams protein, 36 grams carbohydrates, 10 grams total fat, 80 milligrams cholesterol, 156 milligrams sodium.

Ricotta Cheesecake

(Pictured on facing page)
Preparation time: 15 to 20 minutes
Baking time: 55 to 60 minutes
Chilling time: 2 to 3 hours

Calories per serving: 206

Fresh fruit tops this easy-to-make cheesecake. You just blend all the ingredients, then pour the mixture over a wheat-germ-and-butter "crust."

2 **teaspoons butter or margarine, softened**
¼ **cup toasted wheat germ**
3 **eggs**
1½ **pounds (3 cups) ricotta cheese**
⅔ **cup sugar**
⅓ **cup sour cream**
⅓ **cup cornstarch**
1 **teaspoon baking powder**
1 **teaspoon vanilla**
3 **tablespoons butter or margarine, melted and cooled**
2 **teaspoons grated lemon peel**
2 **cups fresh fruit, such as raspberries, strawberries, and/or sliced peaches or nectarines; or Raspberry or Strawberry Sauce (page 40)**
Mint sprigs (optional)

Spread the 2 teaspoons butter over bottom and sides of a 9-inch cake pan with a removable bottom, then sprinkle with wheat germ. Set aside.

In a food processor or blender (or in large bowl of an electric mixer), combine eggs, ricotta cheese, sugar, and sour cream. Whirl (or beat) until smooth. Stir together cornstarch and baking powder; add to cheese mixture along with vanilla, the 3 tablespoons melted butter, and lemon peel. Whirl (or beat) until well blended. Pour into prepared pan.

Bake in a 325° oven until a knife inserted in center comes out clean (55 to 60 minutes). Let cool on a rack, then cover and refrigerate until cold.

To serve, remove pan sides. Arrange some of the fruit attractively on top of cheesecake; garnish with mint, if desired. Offer remaining fruit to accompany individual servings. (Or offer Raspberry or Strawberry Sauce to spoon over individual servings.) Makes 12 servings.

Per serving: 9 grams protein, 18 grams carbohydrates, 11 grams total fat, 98 milligrams cholesterol, 163 milligrams sodium.

Deep-dish Blueberry Pie

Preparation time: about 1½ hours
Baking time: about 40 minutes

Calories per serving: 279

An abundance of fruit with just a little pastry makes this dessert a good choice for those who love the taste of fruit pie but not its calories. The pie has no bottom crust, and pretty pastry cutouts stand in for a solid top crust. This type of pie is a little juicier than traditional double-crust pie, so serve it in bowls. If you like, top each serving with a scoop of Vanilla Frozen Yogurt (page 72).

    Flaky Pastry (recipe follows)
 4 **cups blueberries or huckleberries**
 ¾ **cup sugar**
 3 **tablespoons all-purpose flour**
 ¾ **teaspoon ground cinnamon**
 ¼ **teaspoon ground nutmeg**
 ⅛ **teaspoon salt**
 1 **tablespoon lemon juice**
 1 **egg**
 1 **tablespoon water**

Prepare pastry and refrigerate.

Place blueberries in a large bowl. Add sugar, flour, cinnamon, nutmeg, salt, and lemon juice; stir just until dry ingredients are moistened. Cover blueberry mixture; set aside.

On a lightly floured board, roll out pastry to a thickness of ⅛ inch; cut into decorative shapes with cookie cutters. In a small bowl, lightly beat together egg and water; brush over pastry cutouts.

Spoon blueberry mixture into a rimmed 1-quart baking dish. Lift pastry cutouts with a spatula and place atop blueberry mixture, arranging as desired.

Place a baking sheet on lowest rack of a 450° oven to catch drips; place pie on center rack of oven and bake for 10 minutes. Reduce oven temperature to 350°; continue to bake until pastry is browned (about 30 more minutes). Place pie on a rack and let cool for 15 minutes. To serve, spoon into individual bowls. Makes 6 servings.

Flaky Pastry. In a bowl, stir together ½ cup plus 1 tablespoon **all-purpose flour** and ⅛ teaspoon **salt.** Using a pastry blender or 2 knives, cut in 3 tablespoons **solid vegetable shortening** until particles are about the size of small peas. Pour 1½ tablespoons **cold water** into a cup. Stirring flour mixture lightly and quickly with a fork, sprinkle in water, a little at a time, stirring just until flour is moistened. If mixture seems dry or crumbly, sprinkle in about 1 more teaspoon **cold water;** dough should not be damp or sticky. Stir with a fork until dough clings together and almost cleans sides of bowl.

With your hands, gather dough into a ball; flatten, wrap in plastic wrap, and refrigerate for 1 hour before rolling.

Per serving: 3 grams protein, 51 grams carbohydrates, 8 grams total fat, 46 milligrams cholesterol, 11 milligrams sodium.

Meringue Shells

(Pictured on page 78)
Preparation time: 25 to 35 minutes
Baking time: 1 hour
Drying time: 3 to 4 hours

Calories per shell: 106

Beaten egg whites, lightly sweetened and stabilized with cream of tartar, are easily transformed into crisp, delicate, baked meringue shells—edible containers for fresh fruit, frozen desserts, or no-bake pie fillings. To keep the shells crisp, don't fill them until just before serving; they absorb moisture easily. (For this same reason, it's best not to make meringue shells on a very humid day.)

 4 **egg whites**
 ½ **teaspoon cream of tartar**
 1 **cup sugar**
 1 **teaspoon vanilla**

Cover a baking sheet with plain ungreased brown paper or parchment paper. Trace eight 3½-inch circles on paper, about 1½ inches apart. Set aside.

In large bowl of an electric mixer, beat egg whites with cream of tartar on high speed until foamy. Gradually add sugar, about 1 tablespoon at a time; continue to beat, scraping bowl often, until mixture holds stiff, glossy peaks. Fold in vanilla.

Spoon about ½ cup of the meringue onto each circle on prepared baking sheet. Using back of spoon, spread mixture to cover each circle, then build up a 1½-inch-high rim, creating a hollow in each shell. (Or spoon mixture into a pastry bag fitted with a large star tip; pipe onto traced circles, building up a rim as directed.) Position baking sheet just below center of a 250° oven. Bake for 1 hour; turn off heat and leave in closed oven for 3 to 4 hours to dry.

Remove from oven and let cool completely on baking sheet; then carefully peel off paper backing. If made ahead, store in an airtight container for up to 5 days. Makes 8 shells.

Per shell: 2 grams protein, 25 grams carbohydrates, 0 gram total fat, 0 milligram cholesterol, 25 milligrams sodium.

Lime Angel Pie

Preparation time: 1½ to 2 hours
Chilling time: at least 4 hours

Calories per serving: 169

The term "angel" is often used to describe pies made with a meringue shell rather than a pastry crust, because of the heavenly lightness of the finished product. For this angel pie, the crisp, lightly browned meringue shell is filled with a tangy lime chiffon filling.

For meringue with maximum volume, use large eggs, and have the whites at room temperature before you beat them. (To bring whole eggs to room temperature quickly, cover them with warm water and let stand for 15 minutes.)

    Meringue Shell (recipe follows)
 1 **envelope unflavored gelatin**
 ⅓ **cup lime juice**
 4 **eggs, separated**
 ⅔ **cup water**
 ¾ **cup sugar**
 2 **teaspoons grated lime peel**
 ⅛ **teaspoon salt**
    Few drops of green food color
 ½ **teaspoon cream of tartar**

Prepare Meringue Shell and set aside.

In a small bowl, sprinkle gelatin over lime juice and let stand for about 5 minutes to soften. Meanwhile, in a small pan, lightly beat egg yolks; mix in water, ½ cup of the sugar, lime peel, and salt. Cook over low heat, stirring constantly, until mixture is thick enough to coat a metal spoon in a thin, even layer.

Remove from heat, add gelatin–lime juice mixture, and stir until gelatin is completely dissolved. Add enough food color to tint a medium green. Cover gelatin mixture and refrigerate until thick enough to mound slightly when dropped from a spoon.

In large bowl of an electric mixer, beat egg whites with cream of tartar until foamy; add remaining ¼ cup sugar, 1 tablespoon at a time, and continue to beat until mixture holds stiff peaks. Pour gelatin mixture over egg whites; gently fold together until well combined. Spread mixture evenly in Meringue Shell, cover lightly, and refrigerate until set (several hours) or until next day. Makes 8 servings.

Meringue Shell. In large bowl of an electric mixer, beat 2 **egg whites** and ¼ teaspoon **cream of tartar** until foamy. Add ½ cup **sugar**, 1 tablespoon at a time, beating well after each addition. Continue to beat until sugar is dissolved and meringue holds stiff, glossy peaks.

Spread meringue in a buttered 9-inch pie pan, pushing meringue high on pan sides so it resembles a pie shell. Bake in a 275° oven until lightly browned and dry to the touch (about 50 minutes). Let cool on a rack.

Per serving: 5 grams protein, 32 grams carbohydrates, 3 grams total fat, 137 milligrams cholesterol, 84 milligrams sodium.

Frosty Lemon Torte

Preparation time: 40 to 50 minutes
Freezing time: at least 6 hours

Calories per serving: 221

A coconut crust is the crisp foundation for this creamy delight. Serve it on a summer evening, when cool, refreshing desserts are especially welcome.

    Coconut Crumb Crust (recipe follows)
 2 **eggs, separated**
 ⅔ **cup sugar**
 1 **teaspoon grated lemon peel**
 ⅓ **cup lemon juice**
    Dash of salt
 ⅔ **cup *each* instant nonfat dry milk powder
    and ice water**

Prepare Coconut Crumb Crust, reserving ¼ of the crumb mixture as directed. Set crust aside.

In small bowl of an electric mixer, beat egg yolks until foamy. Gradually add ½ cup of the sugar and continue to beat, scraping bowl often, until thick and lemon-colored. Blend in lemon peel, lemon juice, and salt.

In large bowl of mixer, combine egg whites, dry milk, ice water, and remaining sugar. Beat on high speed until mixture holds stiff peaks (about 5 minutes). Add yolk mixture and beat on low speed just until blended. Pour into crust and sprinkle with reserved crumb mixture.

Cover and freeze until firm (at least 6 hours) or until next day. Remove pan sides and let torte stand at room temperature for 10 minutes before serving. Makes 8 servings.

Coconut Crumb Crust. In a small bowl, stir together 1 cup finely crushed **crisp coconut cookies** and 2 tablespoons **butter** or margarine, melted. Lightly press ¾ of the crumb mixture over bottom of a 9-inch spring-form pan; reserve remaining crumb mixture to garnish top of torte.

Bake crust in a 350° oven until lightly browned (8 to 10 minutes); let cool.

Per serving: 5 grams protein, 33 grams carbohydrates, 9 grams total fat, 98 milligrams cholesterol, 103 milligrams sodium.

Pink Grapefruit Chiffon Pie

(Pictured on facing page)

Preparation time: 1½ to 2 hours
Chilling time: at least 4 hours

Calories per serving: 247

This refreshing pie has the pleasantly tart flavor of grapefruit and the melt-in-your-mouth lightness of chiffon. Because the filling takes time to set, it's ideal for times when you want to get a head start on cooking.

  1 **medium-size pink grapefruit**
  1 **envelope unflavored gelatin**
1½ **cups fresh pink grapefruit juice**
  3 **eggs, separated**
 ¾ **cup sugar**
 ¼ **teaspoon** *each* **salt and grated lemon peel**
 ¼ **cup lemon juice**
 ½ **teaspoon grated pink grapefruit peel**
    Few drops of red food color (optional)
 ¼ **teaspoon cream of tartar**
    Baked 9-inch pastry shell
    Shredded lemon peel or pink grapefruit peel (optional)

Using a sharp knife, cut peel and all white membrane from grapefruit. Cut segments free, lift out, and place in a colander to drain.

In a bowl, sprinkle gelatin over 1 cup of the grapefruit juice and let stand for about 5 minutes to soften. Meanwhile, in a small pan, lightly beat egg yolks; mix in remaining ½ cup grapefruit juice, ½ cup of the sugar, salt, grated lemon peel, lemon juice, and grated grapefruit peel. Cook over low heat, stirring constantly, until mixture is thick enough to coat a metal spoon in a thin, even layer.

Remove from heat, add gelatin–grapefruit juice mixture, and stir until gelatin is completely dissolved. If desired, add enough food color to tint a medium pink. Cover gelatin mixture and refrigerate until thick enough to mound slightly when dropped from a spoon.

In small bowl of an electric mixer, beat egg whites with cream of tartar until foamy; gradually add remaining ¼ cup sugar and continue to beat until mixture holds stiff peaks. Turn chilled gelatin mixture into large bowl of mixer and beat until light and fluffy.

Reserve several of the drained grapefruit segments for garnish; dice remaining segments and fold into gelatin mixture. Then fold in egg white mixture gently but thoroughly.

Spread pie filling evenly in pastry shell, cover lightly, and refrigerate until firm (at least 4 hours) or until next day. Also cover and refrigerate reserved whole grapefruit segments.

To serve, garnish pie with reserved grapefruit segments and, if desired, shredded lemon peel. Makes 8 servings.

Per serving: 5 grams protein, 36 grams carbohydrates, 10 grams total fat, 103 milligrams cholesterol, 234 milligrams sodium.

Watermelon Chiffon Pie

Preparation time: 1½ to 2 hours
Chilling time: at least 6 hours

Calories per serving: 222

Pink, pretty, light, and luscious are the words to describe this airy chiffon pie. Ripe watermelon balls perch on top for a festive garnish. Make your own graham cracker crust, if you like; or use a purchased crust.

    About 3½ pounds ripe watermelon
 ⅓ **cup sugar**
 ⅛ **teaspoon salt**
  1 **envelope unflavored gelatin**
  2 **teaspoons lemon juice**
  2 **egg whites**
 ½ **cup whipping cream**
    9-inch graham cracker crust
    Watermelon balls

Cut off and discard melon rind. Cut fruit into cubes; pick out and discard seeds. Whirl melon cubes in a blender or food processor until smooth. Pour through a fine wire strainer set over a bowl; discard pulp. You should have 1½ cups juice.

Pour melon juice into a pan and stir in sugar and salt. Sprinkle gelatin over juice mixture and let stand for about 5 minutes to soften. Stir over medium heat until gelatin and sugar are completely dissolved, then stir in lemon juice.

Cover gelatin mixture and refrigerate until mixture is thick enough to mound slightly when dropped from a spoon (about 1 hour).

In large bowl of an electric mixer, beat egg whites until they hold stiff peaks; fold in melon mixture. In small bowl of mixer, beat cream until it holds stiff peaks; fold into melon mixture. Spoon into crust.

Cover pie lightly and refrigerate until filling is firm (at least 6 hours). Garnish with watermelon balls before serving. Makes 8 servings.

Per serving: 4 grams protein, 30 grams carbohydrates, 10 grams total fat, 22 milligrams cholesterol, 207 milligrams sodium.

Piquant flavor and feathery-light texture make Pink Grapefruit Chiffon Pie
(recipe on facing page) a dessert to delight your senses.
If you like, you can tint it with food color for a rosier hue.

· ·

Cream Puffs

Preparation time: 25 to 35 minutes
Baking time: about 25 minutes

Calories per medium-size puff: 125

These puffy little pastry shells are marvels of versatility—you can fill them with whatever you like. Try frozen yogurt or fruit as substitutes for the classic (and caloric) ice cream or pastry cream.

  1 cup water
  ½ cup (¼ lb.) butter or margarine
  ¼ teaspoon salt
  1 teaspoon granulated sugar
  1 cup all-purpose flour
  4 eggs
    About 5 cups Vanilla Frozen Yogurt (page 72), purchased frozen yogurt, or sliced fresh fruit
  2 tablespoons powdered sugar

In a 3-quart pan, combine water, butter, salt, and granulated sugar. Bring to a boil over medium-high heat, stirring until butter is melted. Remove pan from heat and add flour all at once. Beat with a wooden spoon until well blended.

Reduce heat to medium. Return pan to heat and stir vigorously with wooden spoon until mixture forms a ball and leaves sides of pan. Remove pan from heat; let mixture cool for 5 minutes. Add eggs, 1 at a time, beating until smooth after each addition. (Mixture will break apart into slippery clumps after each egg is added, but will return to a smooth paste with vigorous beating.)

To shape cream puffs, scoop out batter with a spoon (or spoon batter into a pastry bag fitted with a large plain tip). Use about 2 tablespoons batter for each medium-size puff, about 1 tablespoon for each small puff. Space mounds of batter about 2 inches apart on greased baking sheets.

Bake in upper third of a 425° oven for 15 minutes. Reduce oven temperature to 375°; cut a slash in the bottom of each puff, then continue to bake until puffs are firm, dry to the touch, and golden brown (about 10 more minutes). Transfer to racks and let cool completely. Use puffs as soon as they're cooled; or wrap airtight and let stand at room temperature for up to 24 hours. (Or wrap airtight and freeze for up to 1 month.)

To serve, carefully cut top third from each puff with a sharp knife; scoop out and discard the moist, doughy interior. Spoon filling into puffs. Replace tops and dust with powdered sugar. Makes about 2 dozen medium-size puffs, 3 to 4 dozen small puffs.

Per medium-size puff: 4 grams protein, 14 grams carbohydrates, 6 grams total fat, 81 milligrams cholesterol, 102 milligrams sodium.

Ladyfingers

(Pictured on page 22)
Preparation time: 40 to 45 minutes
Baking time: 9 to 10 minutes

Calories per ladyfinger: 40

If you've never tasted homemade ladyfingers, you're in for a treat: these ethereally light cookies melt in your mouth as their commercially sold cousins never could. Try them with tea and fresh berries for a dainty dessert.

    Cornstarch
  ¾ cup plus 1 tablespoon sifted all-purpose flour
    Dash of salt
  ⅔ cup sugar
  4 eggs, separated
  1 teaspoon vanilla

Grease 2 baking sheets, then dust with cornstarch. (Or use greased, cornstarch-dusted ladyfinger pans.) Set aside.

Sift flour with salt and ⅓ cup of the sugar; set aside.

In large bowl of an electric mixer, beat egg whites until they hold stiff peaks; then gradually beat in remaining ⅓ cup sugar, 1 tablespoon at a time. In small bowl of mixer, beat egg yolks with vanilla until thick and lemon-colored. Fold yolk mixture into egg white mixture. Sift flour mixture over egg mixture; carefully fold in.

Stand a pastry bag fitted with a plain tip (#7 size) in a drinking glass; fill with batter. Pipe batter onto prepared baking sheets, forming fingers about 1 by 4 inches; space fingers about 1 inch apart. (Or spoon batter into ladyfinger pans.)

Bake in a 350° oven until lightly browned (9 to 10 minutes). Let cool on baking sheets (or in pans) for about a minute, then transfer to racks and let cool completely. Store airtight. Makes 2½ dozen ladyfingers.

Per ladyfinger: 1 gram protein, 7 grams carbohydrates, .77 gram total fat, 37 milligrams cholesterol, 14 milligrams sodium.

Won Ton Cinnamon Crisps

Preparation time: 10 to 15 minutes
Baking time: 5 to 6 minutes per panful

Calories per crisp: 27

Cookies made from won ton skins? It may sound strange, but once you try them, you'll be delighted. They take just minutes to make, and the delicate, cinnamon-flavored result is a delicious treat to serve with tea or alongside fruit salad or ice cream.

   20 **won ton skins or 5 egg roll skins**
    3 **to 4 tablespoons butter or margarine, melted**
   ¼ **cup sugar**
    1 **teaspoon ground cinnamon**

Cut each won ton skin in half to make 2 rectangles. (If using egg roll skins, cut each into quarters, then cut each quarter in half to make a total of 8 small rectangles from each skin.)

Brush some of the butter over bottom of a rimmed 10- by 15-inch baking pan. Arrange won ton skins—as many as will fit in a single layer—close together in pan; brush tops with butter. Combine sugar and cinnamon; sprinkle evenly over rectangles.

Bake in a 375° oven until crisp and golden (5 to 6 minutes). Remove from pan; let cool on racks. Repeat to bake remaining won ton skins, using remaining butter and cinnamon-sugar mixture. Makes 40 crisps.

Per crisp: .41 gram protein, 4 grams carbohydrates, 1 gram total fat, 6 milligrams cholesterol, 12 milligrams sodium.

Carob Brownies

(Pictured on page 22)
Preparation time: 20 to 25 minutes
Baking time: about 25 minutes

Calories per brownie: 127

In the Mediterranean region, carob has been a food source for hundreds of years. Only recently, however, have modern cooks come to value it as a more healthful substitute for chocolate. In flavor, color, and aroma, carob is reminiscent of light chocolate, but it's lower in fat and caffeine-free. It's excellent used in baking—try these chewy brownies and see.

    6 **tablespoons butter or margarine**
    2 **eggs**
    1 **cup granulated sugar**
   ½ **teaspoon vanilla**
   ¾ **cup all-purpose flour**
   ½ **cup roasted carob powder**
    1 **teaspoon baking powder**
   ½ **teaspoon salt**
    2 **tablespoons powdered sugar**

Place butter in an 8- or 9-inch square baking pan; set pan in oven while oven preheats to 325°. When butter is melted, remove pan from oven; set aside.

In large bowl of an electric mixer, beat eggs, granulated sugar, and vanilla until thick and lemon-colored; pour in melted butter and stir until blended (set baking pan aside unwashed). In another bowl, stir together flour, carob powder, baking powder, and salt; sift over egg mixture and stir just until smoothly blended.

Spread batter in pan and bake in a 325° oven until a wooden pick inserted in center comes out clean (about 25 minutes). Place pan on a rack and let cool completely. Sift powdered sugar over cooled brownies, then cut into 2- or 2¼-inch squares. Store airtight. Makes 16 brownies.

Per brownie: 2 grams protein, 19 grams carbohydrates, 5 grams total fat, 46 milligrams cholesterol, 151 milligrams sodium.

Greek Lemon Bars

Preparation time: 20 to 25 minutes
Baking time: about 25 minutes

Calories per bar: 70

In a Greek pastry shop, you might find sugar-dusted squares of lemon cake like these. They're meant to be picked up and nibbled like cookies, perhaps with a cup of hot spiced tea or coffee.

    4 **eggs**
    1 **cup granulated sugar**
    1 **teaspoon vanilla**
   ¼ **cup salad oil**
    1 **tablespoon grated lemon peel**
    2 **tablespoons lemon juice**
   ¾ **cup all-purpose flour**
   ⅔ **cup chopped walnuts**
    2 **tablespoons powdered sugar**

In large bowl of an electric mixer, beat eggs and granulated sugar on high speed until about tripled in volume (about 5 minutes). Beat in vanilla, oil, 1 teaspoon of the lemon peel, lemon juice, and flour. Stir in walnuts.

Pour batter into a buttered, flour-dusted 7- by 11-inch baking pan. Bake on center rack of a 375° oven until cake begins to pull from pan sides and center feels set when lightly pressed (about 25 minutes). Let cake cool completely in pan on a rack. If made ahead, cover and let stand at room temperature until next day.

To serve, sift powdered sugar over top of cake and cut into rectangles about 1 by 2 inches. Garnish rectangles with remaining 2 teaspoons lemon peel. Makes about 3 dozen bars.

Per bar: 1 gram protein, 8 grams carbohydrates, 4 grams total fat, 30 milligrams cholesterol, 8 milligrams sodium.

A basketful of assorted cookies makes a tempting dessert that requires no last-minute fuss.
Clockwise from top right, these are Twice-baked Walnut Cookies (facing page),
Mint Meringues (facing page), Ladyfingers (page 20), and Carob Brownies (page 21).

· ·

Mint Meringues

(Pictured on facing page)
Preparation time: 20 to 25 minutes
Baking time: about 1 hour

Calories per cookie: 31

Delightful cookies in their own right, meringues also provide an excellent way for the cook to use up extra egg whites. These dainty meringue morsels, flavored with mint and studded with chocolate chips, add a light touch to your holiday baking. You can tint them green or pink, if you like, which lends them a festive look—and also gives a visual clue to their flavor.

> 2 **egg whites**
> ½ **cup sugar**
> ½ **teaspoon mint extract**
> 6 **to 8 drops green or red food color (optional)**
> 1 **cup regular or miniature semisweet chocolate chips**
> **Additional regular or miniature semisweet chocolate chips (optional)**

In large bowl of an electric mixer, beat egg whites on high speed until foamy. Gradually add sugar, about 1 tablespoon at a time; continue to beat, scraping bowl occasionally, until mixture holds stiff, glossy peaks. Add mint extract; then add food color, if desired. (To make both pink and green meringues, spoon half the uncolored meringue into another bowl; add 3 or 4 drops of green food color to 1 bowl, 3 or 4 drops of red food color to the other.) Beat for 1 more minute; then fold in the 1 cup chocolate chips until evenly combined.

Drop meringue mixture by rounded teaspoonfuls onto well-greased baking sheets, spacing cookies about 1 inch apart. Decorate tops of cookies with additional chocolate chips, if desired. Bake in a 200° oven until outsides of cookies are dry and set (about 1 hour); cookies should not turn brown. Let cool on baking sheets for about 5 minutes, then transfer to racks and let cool completely. Store airtight. Makes about 3½ dozen cookies.

Per cookie: .32 gram protein, 5 grams carbohydrates, 1 gram total fat, 0 milligram cholesterol, 2 milligrams sodium.

Date-Nut Meringues

Follow directions for **Mint Meringues,** but beat a dash of **salt** into egg whites before adding sugar. Omit mint extract, food color, and chocolate chips. Instead, beat in 1 teaspoon **vanilla;** then fold in 1 cup *each* chopped **pitted dates** and finely chopped **walnuts.**

Twice-baked Walnut Cookies

(Pictured on facing page)
Preparation time: 30 to 40 minutes
Baking time: about 35 minutes

Calories per cookie: 40

Here's a way to make a large batch of crunchy cookies with a minimum of fuss. The dough goes together in one big bowl, then is rolled into ropes and baked. Cut the ropes into slices, bake again, and you've got 12 dozen delicious, nut-flavored treats to enjoy with coffee for a simple dessert.

> 4 **eggs**
> 1½ **cups sugar**
> ¾ **cup (¼ lb. plus ¼ cup) butter or margarine, melted**
> 2 **teaspoons vanilla**
> 1 **teaspoon** *each* **anise extract and black walnut flavoring**
> ½ **teaspoon almond extract**
> 1 **cup chopped walnuts**
> 5 **cups all-purpose flour**
> 4½ **teaspoons baking powder**

In a large bowl, beat eggs and sugar with a heavy spoon until well blended. Stir in butter, vanilla, anise extract, black walnut flavoring, almond extract, and walnuts.

Mix flour and baking powder; gradually stir into butter mixture, blending well. Scrape dough out onto a floured board and divide into 8 equal portions. With your hands, roll each portion into a 14-inch-long rope. Place ropes about 2 inches apart on greased 12- by 15-inch baking sheets.

Bake in a 325° oven until bottoms of ropes are pale golden (about 20 minutes). Let cool on baking sheets for about 2 minutes, then cut each rope diagonally into ½- to ¾-inch-thick slices.

Tip slices onto their cut sides; arrange close together on baking sheets. Increase oven temperature to 375° and bake cookies until lightly toasted (about 15 minutes). Let cool on baking sheets. Store airtight at room temperature for up to 1 month; freeze for longer storage. Makes about 12 dozen cookies.

Per cookie: .73 gram protein, 6 grams carbohydrates, 2 grams total fat, 10 milligrams cholesterol, 25 milligrams sodium.

Twice-baked Fruit Cookies

Follow directions for **Twice-baked Walnut Cookies,** but omit black walnut flavoring. In place of walnuts, use ¾ cup diced **mixed candied fruit** and ¼ cup **pine nuts** or slivered almonds.

Fresh Fruit Delights

NATURALLY SWEET & JUICY

When you're looking for light desserts, fresh fruits in season are an obvious choice. Flavorful, juicy, low in fat and calories, and high in vitamins and fiber, they're a healthful way to appease a sweet tooth.

In the following recipes, you'll find many ideas for enhancing fresh fruit without obscuring its natural flavor. And if you wish, you can add even simpler embellishments to create ultra-light, extra-easy desserts. A squeeze of lemon or lime juice adds sophisticated flavor at only 4 calories per tablespoon; a light sprinkling of toasted sliced almonds or shredded coconut dresses up plain fruit without substantially boosting calorie count. You might also try topping your favorite fruit with a little honey, brown sugar, or powdered sugar, then serving it at room temperature or broiling it briefly.

Cracked Caramel Apples in Chaudeau

Preparation time: 30 to 40 minutes
Baking time: about 1 hour

Calories per serving: 266

The foamy European dessert called *chaudeau* usually is served as a beverage, but it also makes a wonderful sauce. In this case, it's poured around baked apples glazed with caramel syrup. The resulting dessert offers an appealing contrast of flavors and textures.

    6 **Newtown Pippin apples, peeled and cored**
    2 **tablespoons butter or margarine**
    ½ **cup plus 1½ teaspoons sugar**
    2 **tablespoons water**
      Chaudeau (page 93)

Set apples upright and slightly apart in a 7- by 11-inch baking pan. Place 1 teaspoon of the butter on each apple, then sprinkle each with ¼ teaspoon of the sugar. Cover and bake in a 350° oven until apples are tender when pierced (about 1 hour). With 2 spoons, lift apples from pan and place each on a rimmed dessert plate or in a wide, shallow bowl. Use apples hot or cooled.

In a wide frying pan, combine water and remaining ½ cup sugar. Bring to a boil over high heat. Then continue to boil, uncovered, stirring constantly, until syrup is a deep amber color (about 5 minutes; sugar will crystallize, but with constant stirring it will liquefy again). Immediately pour hot syrup over apples, dividing equally. At once prepare Chaudeau and pour equally over apples. Serve immediately. Makes 6 servings.

Per serving: 2 grams protein, 47 grams carbohydrates, 6 grams total fat, 101 milligrams cholesterol, 64 milligrams sodium.

Cider-poached Apples with Yogurt

Preparation time: 30 to 40 minutes
Cooking time: 8 to 15 minutes

Calories per serving: 300

The flavors of autumn take center stage here. Cored whole apples are poached to tenderness in an apple cider syrup, then topped with yogurt and chopped pecans. For an extra-special flavor, toast the chopped nuts in the oven until lightly browned.

    4 **cups apple cider or juice**
    4 **medium-size McIntosh or Golden Delicious apples**
    ½ **to ¾ cup plain or berry-flavored lowfat yogurt**
    ½ **cup chopped pecans**

In a 2- to 3-quart pan, bring cider to a boil over high heat; continue to boil, uncovered, until reduced to 1 cup.

Peel apples, if desired; then cut out and discard cores. Add cored apples to cider. Bring to a boil; reduce heat, cover, and simmer until apples are tender when pierced (8 to 15 minutes). Serve apples and sauce in individual bowls; spoon yogurt and pecans equally over fruit. Makes 4 servings.

Per serving: 4 grams protein, 53 grams carbohydrates, 10 grams total fat, 3 milligrams cholesterol, 37 milligrams sodium.

Chunky Applesauce

Preparation time: 20 to 30 minutes
Cooking time: 45 to 50 minutes

Calories per serving: 281

An apple a day may not keep the doctor away—but then again, it may. In either case, apples certainly do make delicious and healthful desserts; this thick, cinnamon-scented applesauce is proof enough.

   10 **large apples, such as Gravenstein or Golden Delicious (about 5 lbs. *total*), peeled, cored, and sliced (about 14 cups *total*)**
    2 **cups water**
    ½ **to ¾ cup sugar**
    1 **teaspoon ground cinnamon**

In a 6- to 8-quart pan, combine apples, water, and ½ cup of the sugar. Cook, uncovered, over medium heat until mixture begins to splatter (about 15 minutes); stir several times. Sprinkle cinnamon over apples. Reduce heat, cover, and simmer until apples mash readily (about 30 minutes), stirring about every 10 minutes. Taste halfway through cooking; add up to ¼ cup more sugar, if desired.

Remove from heat. With a heavy spoon, break up and coarsely mash apples; sauce should be chunky. Return to heat and simmer, uncovered, until slightly thickened (3 to 5 more minutes). Serve warm or cooled. If made ahead, cover cooled applesauce and refrigerate for up to 1 week. Makes 6 servings (about 6 cups *total*).

Per serving: .49 gram protein, 73 grams carbohydrates, 1 gram total fat, 0 milligram cholesterol, .34 milligram sodium.

Soufflé-topped Baked Apples

Preparation time: 40 to 50 minutes
Baking time: 55 to 65 minutes

Calories per serving: 238

For a simple yet delightful dessert, it's hard to improve on a perfect apple—crisp, sweet, juicy, and satisfying. And apples are delicious cooked, too, whether poached or made into sauce (see page 25), served up as a homey apple crisp (see page 28), or baked.

Here, old-fashioned baked apples take on a new look: the fruit is filled with apricot jam, topped with a light, lemony soufflé mixture, and baked until puffy and golden brown. If you like, substitute raspberry jam or perhaps orange marmalade for the apricot jam.

   8 **medium-size Golden Delicious apples, peeled and cored**
   2 **tablespoons lemon juice**
   8 **teaspoons apricot jam**
   2 **tablespoons cornstarch**
1¾ **cups lowfat milk**
   4 **eggs, separated**
   1 **teaspoon grated lemon peel**
   ¾ **cup sugar**

Set apples upright and slightly apart in a 9- by 13-inch baking dish. Sprinkle with lemon juice. Cover and bake in a 350° oven until apples are tender when pierced (40 to 50 minutes). Remove from oven; drain off and discard pan juices. Fill each apple with 1 teaspoon of the jam; set apples aside. Increase oven temperature to 400°.

Place cornstarch in a 1- to 1½-quart pan. Gradually add milk, stirring until smoothly blended; then bring to a full boil, stirring. Remove from heat. In a small bowl, beat egg yolks and lemon peel until blended. Add some of the hot milk mixture, beating constantly; then pour egg mixture back into pan. Cook over low heat, stirring constantly, for 1 minute. Set aside.

In large bowl of an electric mixer, beat egg whites until foamy; gradually add sugar and continue to beat until mixture holds stiff peaks. Fold custard into egg white mixture, then spoon mixture evenly over apples in baking dish. Bake, uncovered, until topping is lightly browned (about 15 minutes). Serve warm. Makes 8 servings.

Per serving: 5 grams protein, 47 grams carbohydrates, 4 grams total fat, 141 milligrams cholesterol, 63 milligrams sodium.

Crumb-coated Apples

(Pictured on facing page)
Preparation time: 30 to 40 minutes
Baking time: about 1 hour

Calories per serving: 256

After an autumn dinner, everyone is sure to enjoy this warm apple dessert. The fruit is filled with orange marmalade and cloaked in sweet crumbs, then baked until tender. Offer our low-calorie Whipped Topping, softly whipped cream, or Vanilla Frozen Yogurt alongside, if you wish.

   ⅔ **cup fine soft bread crumbs**
   ⅓ **cup *each* firmly packed brown sugar and finely chopped almonds**
   6 **large Rome Beauty apples or other firm cooking apples, peeled and cored**
   2 **egg whites, lightly beaten**
   6 **tablespoons orange marmalade**
   ¾ **cup apple juice or white port**
       Mint sprigs (optional)
       Whipped Topping (page 41), whipped cream, or Vanilla Frozen Yogurt (page 72), optional

In a small bowl, combine crumbs, sugar, and almonds. Brush apples all over with egg whites, then roll in crumb mixture to coat evenly. Arrange apples upright, sides not touching, in a 7- by 11-inch baking pan. Spoon 1 tablespoon of the marmalade into the cavity of each apple. Pour apple juice around apples in pan.

Bake, uncovered, in a 350° oven until apples are tender when pierced (about 1 hour). Serve warm or at room temperature.

To serve, place 1 apple on each of 6 individual rimmed plates; leave apples whole or cut in slices to reveal the marmalade filling. Garnish apples with mint and offer Whipped Topping to accompany fruit, if desired. Makes 6 servings.

Per serving: 3 grams protein, 55 grams carbohydrates, 4 grams total fat, .20 milligram cholesterol, 50 milligrams sodium.

Cinnamon & Walnut Crumb-coated Apples

Follow directions for **Crumb-coated Apples,** but substitute finely chopped **walnuts** for almonds. Add ½ teaspoon **ground cinnamon** to the crumb mixture before coating apples; substitute **apricot jam** for orange marmalade.

A sweet spoonful of orange marmalade fills center of Crumb-coated Apples (recipe
on facing page). This satisfying winter dessert can be
served warm or at room temperature, plain or with a creamy topping.

· ·

Golden Apple Crisp

Preparation time: 25 to 35 minutes
Baking time: about 40 minutes

Calories per serving: 174

Concealed under a crunchy cinnamon topping, sliced apples bake to sweet succulence in apricot nectar or orange juice. Serve this homey dessert warm or cold.

  4 or 5 medium-size Golden Delicious apples (about 1½ lbs. *total*), peeled, cored, and cut into ½-inch-thick slices (6 cups *total*)
⅓ **cup apricot nectar or orange juice**
¼ **cup granulated sugar**
½ **cup firmly packed brown sugar**
¾ **teaspoon ground cinnamon**
¼ **teaspoon salt**
¾ **cup all-purpose flour**
¼ **cup firm butter or margarine**

Distribute apples evenly in a well-buttered 7- by 11-inch baking dish.

In a bowl, combine apricot nectar and granulated sugar; pour over apples. In another bowl, mix brown sugar, cinnamon, salt, and flour until well blended. Using a pastry blender or 2 knives, cut butter into flour mixture until particles are about the size of peas. Sprinkle crumb mixture evenly over apples.

Bake, uncovered, in a 375° oven until topping is browned and apples are tender when pierced (about 40 minutes). Serve warm; or let cool completely, then cover, refrigerate, and serve cold. Makes 6 to 8 servings.

Per serving: .19 gram protein, 32 grams carbohydrates, 6 grams total fat, 16 milligrams cholesterol, 131 milligrams sodium.

Frozen Yogurt Bananas

(Pictured on page 46)
Preparation time: 20 to 30 minutes
Freezing time: about 2 hours

Calories per serving: 128

Coated in creamy, nutritious, honey-flavored yogurt and rolled in toasted coconut, this familiar fruit on a stick can wait in the freezer for a special snack, family dessert, or children's party.

Use firm, green-tipped bananas to make this treat. Once the coating is firmly set, cover the

bananas tightly and store them in the freezer; they'll keep well for about 2 weeks.

1 **cup plain lowfat yogurt**
¼ **cup honey**
5 **medium-size firm, green-tipped bananas**
1 **cup sweetened flaked coconut, unsweetened grated coconut, or chopped almonds**

In a small bowl, blend yogurt and honey. Peel bananas; cut in half crosswise and insert a flat wooden stick into cut end of each half.

Dip banana halves in yogurt mixture to coat completely. Place banana halves slightly apart on a baking sheet lined with wax paper. Cover with plastic wrap and freeze until coating is firm (about 1 hour).

Meanwhile, spread coconut or almonds on a baking sheet and toast in a 350° oven until golden (8 to 10 minutes), stirring often. Let cool.

Dip each banana in yogurt mixture again, then roll in coconut or almonds. Return to wax paper-lined baking sheet, cover, and freeze until coating is firm. Before serving, let stand at room temperature for about 5 minutes. Makes 10 servings.

Per serving: 2 grams protein, 25 grams carbohydrates, 3 grams total fat, 1 milligram cholesterol, 36 milligrams sodium.

Fruit-flavored Frozen Yogurt Bananas

Follow directions for **Frozen Yogurt Bananas,** but omit plain yogurt and honey; instead, use 1 cup **fruit-flavored lowfat yogurt,** stirred well.

Broiled Bananas & Pineapple

Preparation time: 10 to 20 minutes
Broiling time: 5 to 7 minutes

Calories per serving: 214

This hot fruit dessert is an excellent choice for the chilly months when other fresh fruit is scarce. Pineapple and bananas are broiled with brown sugar and butter, then topped with cool sour cream.

3 **ripe bananas**
6 **slices fresh or drained canned pineapple**
⅓ **cup firmly packed brown sugar**
2 **tablespoons butter or margarine**
1 **tablespoon lemon juice**
½ **cup sour cream**

Peel each banana and cut in half crosswise, then lengthwise, to make 4 pieces (you will have 12 pieces *total*).

Arrange bananas and pineapple in a single layer in a baking dish. Sprinkle with sugar, dot with butter, and sprinkle with lemon juice. Broil about 8 inches below heat until fruit is glazed (5 to 7 minutes), basting several times. While fruit is still hot, arrange 2 pieces of banana and 1 pineapple slice in each of 6 dessert dishes. Top servings equally with sour cream; spoon some of the hot butter sauce over sour cream. Makes 6 servings.

Per serving: 2 grams protein, 36 grams carbohydrates, 8 grams total fat, 19 milligrams cholesterol, 55 milligrams sodium.

Broiled Orange Halves

Preparation time: about 10 minutes
Broiling time: about 3 minutes

Calories per serving: 70

Though usually served chilled, fresh oranges make a delightful dessert when warm. Here, they're topped with brown sugar, sherry, and butter, then run under the broiler until bubbly.

3 large oranges
1 tablespoon *each* firmly packed brown sugar and dry sherry
1 tablespoon butter or margarine, melted

Cut oranges in half crosswise. Using a grapefruit knife, carefully cut around fruit in each half to separate it from peel and membrane, but leave fruit in shells. Then arrange orange halves in an 8- or 9-inch square baking pan; sprinkle each orange half with ½ teaspoon *each* of the sugar, sherry, and butter. Broil 4 inches below heat until hot and bubbly (about 3 minutes). Serve warm; eat fruit from shell with a spoon. Makes 6 servings.

Per serving: .68 gram protein, 13 grams carbohydrates, 2 grams total fat, 5 milligrams cholesterol, 20 milligrams sodium.

Orange Ambrosia

Preparation time: 15 to 20 minutes
Chilling time: at least 2 hours

Calories per serving: 174

The dessert called ambrosia is named for the food of the Greek and Roman gods; in fact, its name comes from the Greek word meaning "immortality." The ancients believed that their gods feasted on this delectable dish in a celestial abode on Mount Olympus. Today, ambrosia refers to a sweet fruit salad made with oranges and shredded coconut.

2 large oranges
1 large banana
1 cup seedless red or green grapes
2 teaspoons lemon juice
¼ to ⅓ cup sugar
¼ cup sweetened or unsweetened flaked coconut

Using a sharp knife, cut peel and all white membrane from oranges. Hold fruit over a large bowl to catch juice; cut segments free, lift out, and place in bowl. Cut banana into ½-inch-thick slices. Add to bowl along with grapes and lemon juice; toss. Sprinkle sugar and coconut over fruit; cover and refrigerate for at least 2 hours to blend flavors. Makes 4 servings.

Per serving: 1 gram protein, 41 grams carbohydrates, 2 grams total fat, 0 milligram cholesterol, 13 milligrams sodium.

Fresh Orange Cups

Preparation time: 10 to 15 minutes
Chilling time: 2 to 3 hours

Calories per serving: 97

Like melon and pineapple, oranges can provide you with both a sweet, juicy light dessert and an attractive "dish" to serve it in. Here, you remove the fruit from halved oranges, toss it with liqueur, and pile it back into the shells. After chilling, the self-contained little desserts are whisked right to the table.

5 to 7 large oranges
4 to 6 tablespoons orange- or almond-flavored liqueur

Cut 3 or 4 of the oranges in half crosswise. Using a grapefruit knife, carefully cut around fruit in each half to separate it from peel and membrane. Lift out fruit from each orange half. Hold fruit over a large bowl to catch juice; cut segments free, lift out, and drop into bowl. Using a sharp knife, cut peel and all white membrane from remaining 2 or 3 oranges; cut segments free, lift out, and place in bowl. Sprinkle liqueur over oranges; toss gently to coat. Pile fruit equally into orange shells, cover, and refrigerate until cold (2 to 3 hours). Serve cold. Makes 6 to 8 servings.

Per serving: 1 gram protein, 21 grams carbohydrates, .34 gram total fat, 0 milligram cholesterol, 0 milligram sodium.

This light, sparkling dessert is a celebration in itself! Oranges in Ginger Champagne
(recipe on facing page) features cold ginger syrup,
fresh orange segments, and a generous splash of dry champagne.

• •

Oranges in Ginger Champagne

(Pictured on facing page)

Preparation time: 30 to 40 minutes
Chilling time: 4 to 5 hours

Calories per serving: 207

After a Chinese dinner—or whenever you want a dessert that's light and refreshing—offer fresh orange segments in a cold ginger syrup, spooned into wine glasses and splashed with chilled champagne.

- ¾ **cup** *each* **sugar and water**
- 2 **tablespoons minced crystallized ginger**
- 4 **large oranges**
- 1 **bottle (about 750 ml.) dry champagne or 3 to 4 cups ginger ale**

In a 2- to 3-quart pan, combine sugar, water, and ginger. Stir over medium heat until sugar is dissolved; then bring to a boil over high heat and continue to boil, uncovered, for 5 minutes. Let cool, then refrigerate until cold or until next day.

Using a sharp knife, cut peel and all white membrane from oranges. Hold oranges over pan of cold ginger syrup to catch juice; cut segments free, lift out, and add to cold syrup. Stir gently. Cover and refrigerate for about 3 hours.

To serve, spoon oranges and syrup equally into 6 to 8 champagne or wine glasses. Pour champagne over fruit to fill glasses. Makes 6 to 8 servings.

Per serving: .76 gram protein, 37 grams carbohydrates, .19 gram total fat, 0 milligram cholesterol, 7 milligrams sodium.

Oranges Casablanca

Preparation time: 15 to 20 minutes
Chilling time: at least 2 hours

Calories per serving: 122

Casablanca . . . the very name of Morocco's largest city is enough to fire the imagination. This Moroccan dessert is intriguing, too—very simple, but exotically flavored with fragrant orange flower water.

- 4 **large oranges**
- 2 **tablespoons** *each* **sugar and water**
- 1 **teaspoon orange flower water**
- 1 **tablespoon chopped pistachio nuts, almonds, or walnuts**

Using a sharp knife, cut peel and all white membrane from oranges. Hold fruit over a large bowl to catch juice; cut segments free, lift out, and place in bowl. In a small bowl, mix sugar, water, and orange flower water; drizzle over oranges, then cover and refrigerate for at least 2 hours to blend flavors.

To serve, spoon oranges and juice equally into 4 dessert dishes; top equally with pistachio nuts. Makes 4 servings.

Per serving: 2 grams protein, 28 grams carbohydrates, 1 gram total fat, 0 milligram cholesterol, .18 milligram sodium.

Feijoas in Orange Syrup

Preparation time: 20 to 30 minutes
Chilling time: at least 3 hours

Calories per serving: 145

Oval, olive-green feijoas (pineapple guavas) are one of the less familiar autumn fruits—but they're well worth sampling. To make this simple dessert, you pare off the feijoas' sour skin, then cut the fruit crosswise to reveal the decorative pattern of seeds. The slices are then chilled in a fresh orange syrup that perfectly complements their sweet-tart flavor.

For the orange peel, juice, and segments called for in the recipe, you'll need a total of three or four large oranges. Cut the peel from one orange, using a sharp knife or vegetable peeler; then squeeze the peeled fruit plus another orange to make 1 cup juice. Cut the segments from one or two more oranges— you need 1 cup total.

- 1 **cup orange juice**
  Peel cut from 1 large orange (orange part only)
- ½ **cup sugar**
- ¼ **cup water**
- 4 **or 5 feijoas**
- 1 **cup orange segments**

In a 1- to 2-quart pan, combine orange juice, orange peel, sugar, and water. Bring to a boil over high heat; continue to boil rapidly, uncovered, until syrup is reduced to 1 cup. Remove from heat.

Using a vegetable peeler or a sharp knife, peel feijoas; then cut crosswise into ¼-inch-thick slices. Drop slices into hot orange syrup; add orange segments and mix gently. Cover and refrigerate until cold or until next day. To serve, spoon fruit and syrup into dessert bowls. Makes 4 or 5 servings.

Per serving: .93 gram protein, 36 grams carbohydrates, .17 gram total fat, 0 milligram cholesterol, 1 milligram sodium.

For those who love candy but also value the fresh flavor and wholesomeness of fruit, here are confections that offer the best of both worlds. They'll satisfy any sweet tooth, but are lighter and more nutritious than most commercial candies.

Our recipes offer a number of choices. If it's holiday time, perhaps you'll want to make our chewy Cranberry Candy for a special gift. Apple lovers will want to try the Apple-Walnut Candy— it's something like Turkish delight. Chewy Strawberry Caramels and Apricot Slims make excellent after-dinner treats or snacks. And for fans of fresh fruit, we've included Chocolate-striped Oranges and Frosted Kiwi Slices & Berries.

Apple-Walnut Candy

1½ pounds Golden
  Delicious apples (4 or
  5 medium-size)
2 tablespoons water
2 cups granulated sugar
2 envelopes unflavored
  gelatin
2 teaspoons rose water
  (optional)
1 teaspoon *each* grated
  lemon peel and lemon
  juice
½ teaspoon almond extract
1½ cups chopped walnuts
½ cup powdered sugar

Core unpeeled apples and cut into 1-inch chunks; you should have about 6 cups. In a 3- to 4-quart pan, combine apples and water; bring to a simmer, then cover and simmer over medium-low heat until tender when pierced. Uncover and cook briefly, stirring occasionally, until excess liquid has evaporated.

Turn apples into a blender or food processor and whirl until almost smooth; then return to pan. Stir together granulated sugar and gelatin; stir into apples. Bring to a boil; then reduce heat slightly and boil gently, uncovered, stirring, until you can see pan bottom for a full second after spoon is drawn across bottom (15 to 18 minutes).

Remove apple mixture from heat and stir in rose water (if used), lemon peel, lemon juice, almond extract, and walnuts. Pour into a well-buttered 8- or 9-inch square baking dish; let cool, then cover and let stand at room temperature until next day.

Cut candy into 1-inch squares, remove from dish with a spatula, and place, slightly apart, on racks. Let dry, uncovered, for 8 to 12 hours, then dust with powdered sugar. Store, loosely covered, at room temperature for up to 2 weeks. Makes 64 or 81 pieces.

Strawberry Caramels

1 package (16 oz.) frozen
  unsweetened
  strawberries, thawed
2¼ cups sugar
1 cup whipping cream
1 cup ice water
  Salad oil

Whirl strawberries and their juice in a food processor or blender until puréed. In a heavy 4- to 5-quart pan, stir together purée, sugar, and cream. Cook over high heat, uncovered. Stir often at first; then, as mixture thickens, stir constantly to prevent scorching. When mixture registers about 240°F on a candy thermometer, test consistency: drop ¼ teaspoon into ice water and roll into a ball

between your fingers. The texture should be like soft caramel; if mixture is too soft, continue to cook. Total cooking time will be 15 to 20 minutes.

Pour mixture into a well-buttered 9- by 13-inch pan, spreading evenly with a spatula; let cool to room temperature (about 20 minutes). With scissors dipped in oil, cut candy into 1-inch squares. Wrap each piece in a 4-inch square of wax paper. Store airtight at room temperature for up to 1 week. Makes about 10 dozen pieces.

Cranberry Candy

2 cups (½ lb.) fresh or
  frozen cranberries
1½ tablespoons grated
  orange peel
¾ cup orange juice
3 envelopes unflavored
  gelatin
1½ cups sugar
1 cup chopped walnuts

In a 2- to 3-quart pan, combine cranberries, orange peel, and orange juice. Cover and cook over medium-high heat until cranberries soften and pop open (about 15 minutes). Let cool.

Whirl mixture, a portion at a time, in a blender or food processor until smooth; then force through a fine wire strainer. Discard residue.

Return cranberry purée to pan. Stir together gelatin and sugar; add to cranberry purée and stir until sugar is dissolved. Cook over medium-high heat, stirring, until you can see pan bottom for a full second after spoon is drawn across bottom (10 to 12 minutes). Remove from heat; stir in walnuts.

Spread mixture evenly in a well-buttered 5- by 9-inch loaf pan and let stand, uncovered, for at least 8 hours. Cut into 1-inch squares and arrange, slightly apart, on a rack. Let dry, uncovered, for 8 to 12 hours (candy will be moist-dry). Makes 45 pieces.

Apricot Slims

1 cup moist-pack dried apricots

⅓ cup unsweetened grated coconut

1 tablespoon orange juice

¼ cup finely chopped almonds

If apricots aren't moist, place in a wire strainer and steam over simmering water for 5 minutes.

Put apricots through a food chopper fitted with a fine blade. Then combine chopped apricots with coconut and put through food chopper again. Add orange juice and mix well. Divide mixture into 4 equal portions, wrap in plastic wrap, and refrigerate until well chilled.

Work with 1 portion of apricot mixture at a time. On a board, roll each portion back and forth with the palms of your hands to form a 16-inch-long rope. For each rope, sprinkle board with 1 tablespoon of the almonds; roll rope in almonds to coat. Cut each rope diagonally into 2-inch pieces. Makes 32 pieces.

Pear Slims

Follow directions for **Apricot Slims,** but substitute 6 ounces (about 1 cup) **dried pears** for apricots; remove any bits of stem or core from pears. Instead of orange juice, use 1 tablespoon

lemon juice; instead of almonds, use ¼ cup **unsweetened grated coconut.**

Chocolate-striped Oranges

2 large navel oranges

8 ounces semisweet chocolate

About 2 tablespoons solid vegetable shortening

3 ounces white chocolate or white pastel coating

Carefully peel oranges and separate into segments without breaking membrane. Pull off all loose pith and white fibers.

In the top of a narrow double boiler over water just below simmering, combine semisweet chocolate and 1 teaspoon of the shortening. When chocolate begins to soften, stir until smooth. Remove from heat but keep over hot water.

Tilt pan to make deepest pool of chocolate possible. Dip each orange segment into chocolate, coating half of segment. Set segments upright, sides not touching, on a tray lined with wax paper. Refrigerate just until chocolate is firm (about 10 minutes). Save remaining chocolate for other uses.

Wash and dry top of double boiler. Put in white chocolate and ½ teaspoon of the shortening. Set over water just below simmering; when chocolate begins to soften, stir until smooth. If needed, stir in up to 1½ tablespoons more shortening to achieve drizzling consistency. Remove from heat but keep over hot water.

Hold each orange segment by uncoated end over white choco-

late; dip tines of a fork into white chocolate, then drizzle in a quick steady motion over dark chocolate to make thin stripes.

Return segments to tray; refrigerate just until coating is firm. Serve; or cover loosely with plastic wrap and refrigerate for up to 4 hours. Allow 3 orange segments per person. Makes 6 to 8 servings.

Frosted Kiwi Slices & Berries

2 firm-ripe kiwi fruit

10 to 12 large strawberries

4 ounces white chocolate or white pastel coating

1 teaspoon solid vegetable shortening, if needed

Peel kiwi and cut into thick slices. Place on paper towels and let stand, turning often, until excess juice is absorbed. Wash strawberries but do not hull; let dry on paper towels.

Place white chocolate in the top of a double boiler set over water just below simmering; when chocolate begins to soften, stir until smooth. If too thick, add shortening and stir until melted. Remove from heat but keep over hot water.

Tilt pan to make deepest pool of chocolate possible. Dip each kiwi slice about halfway into chocolate and place on a tray lined with wax paper. Hold each strawberry by top, dip tip about halfway into chocolate, and set on tray with kiwi. Refrigerate, uncovered, until coating is hardened (at least 30 minutes) or for up to 4 hours. Serve cold. Makes about 24 pieces (6 to 8 servings).

Berries in Frosted Glasses

Preparation time: about 1 hour

Calories per serving: 76

Plump, fresh berries need little adornment to make a delicious seasonal dessert. Here, they're merely sweetened to taste and served with a touch of something creamy in chilled, sugar-frosted glasses.

> 3 **egg whites**
> **Sugar**
> 2 **cups blackberries, raspberries, or blueberries**
> ½ **cup Whipped Topping (page 41), whipped cream, sour cream, or honey-sweetened plain lowfat yogurt**

In small bowl of an electric mixer, beat egg whites until frothy. Fill another small bowl with sugar. Choose four 6- to 8-ounce stemmed glasses; invert each glass and dip top inch of rim into egg whites, then into sugar. Refrigerate glasses until very cold.

Place ½ cup of the berries in each glass; sprinkle each serving with 1 teaspoon sugar, then top with 2 tablespoons of the Whipped Topping. Makes 4 servings.

Per serving: 4 grams protein, 12 grams carbohydrates, 2 grams total fat, .32 milligram cholesterol, 48 milligrams sodium.

Raspberries Under a Cloud

(Pictured on facing page)
Preparation time: 25 to 35 minutes
Broiling time: about 2 minutes

Calories per serving: 151

The fragile juiciness of warm raspberries is emphasized in this dramatic dessert. Crowned with a billowy cloud of meringue and surrounded by a piquant fresh orange sauce, the berries make a bright and flavorful display.

> **Orange Sauce (recipe follows)**
> 2 **cups raspberries**
> 3 **egg whites**
> 1 **teaspoon vanilla**
> ¼ **teaspoon cream of tartar**
> ½ **cup granulated sugar**
> 3 **tablespoons powdered sugar**

Prepare Orange Sauce and set aside.

Place raspberries in a single layer in center of a 10- to 12-inch rimmed ovenproof serving plate (or a decorative tart pan).

In large bowl of an electric mixer, combine egg whites, vanilla, and cream of tartar. Beat on high speed until frothy. Gradually add granulated sugar and continue to beat until mixture holds stiff peaks.

Spoon meringue into a pastry bag fitted with a large star tip; pipe over raspberries, leaving a 1-inch border of berries. (Or swirl meringue over berries with a spoon.) Sift powdered sugar evenly over top. Broil 6 inches below heat until lightly browned (about 2 minutes). Pour Orange Sauce around raspberries (not on meringue). Serve hot or slightly warm. Makes 6 to 8 servings.

Orange Sauce. In a 1- to 1½-quart pan, stir together ½ cup **sugar** and 1½ tablespoons **cornstarch.** Blend in 1 cup **orange juice** and 1 thin slice *each* of **orange** and **lemon** (including peel), cut into quarters. Stir over high heat until sauce boils and thickens. Remove from heat; stir in 3 tablespoons **lemon juice.** Use warm or cooled. If made ahead, cover and store at room temperature for up to several hours.

Per serving: 2 grams protein, 37 grams carbohydrates, .18 gram total fat, 0 milligram cholesterol, 21 milligrams sodium.

Fruit with Yogurt & Caramelized Sugar

Preparation time: 10 to 15 minutes

Calories per serving: 114

A sweet, crisp, lacy-looking veil of caramelized sugar adorns the fruit and yogurt in this attractive dessert. The recipe serves two, but can easily be multiplied for additional servings.

> 1 **cup plain lowfat yogurt**
> 6 **to 8 large strawberries, hulled; or 4 small apricots, halved and pitted; or 2 small peaches, halved and pitted**
> 1½ **tablespoons sugar**

Divide yogurt equally between 2 small, shallow serving bowls. Set 3 or 4 strawberries (or 4 apricot halves or 2 peach halves) on yogurt in each dish.

Place sugar in a 6-inch frying pan or a 1-quart or smaller pan. Cook over medium heat just until sugar is melted and amber-colored; tilt and shake pan often to mix sugar as it begins to liquefy and caramelize. Let cool until thickened to the consistency of a light syrup (about 1 minute). Slowly drizzle caramelized sugar over fruit and yogurt in a thin, steady stream, then serve. Makes 2 servings.

Per serving: 6 grams protein, 19 grams carbohydrates, 2 grams total fat, 7 milligrams cholesterol, 80 milligrams sodium.

A lavish swirl of meringue is the crowning touch for Raspberries
Under a Cloud (recipe on facing page).
A piquant orange sauce complements the berries' fresh flavor.

· ·

Strawberries in Wine

Preparation time: 20 to 25 minutes
Chilling time: at least 4 hours

Calories per serving: 142

When sweetened, heated, and lightly thickened, muscat wine makes a superb sauce for fresh strawberries. Serve this make-ahead dessert plain or topped with a dollop of sour cream.

>   8 **cups strawberries, hulled and halved lengthwise**
> 1⅔ **cups muscat wine or sweet sherry**
>   ¾ **cup sugar**
>   2 **tablespoons cornstarch**
>   **Sour cream, Whipped Topping (page 41), or whipped cream (optional)**

Place strawberries in a deep bowl and pour in wine; toss to coat. Cover and refrigerate for at least 2 hours.

In a small pan, stir together sugar and cornstarch. Drain strawberries, reserving liquid; gradually add liquid to cornstarch mixture, stirring until smooth. Cook over high heat, stirring constantly, just until mixture boils and thickens; let cool completely. Pour cooled wine mixture over berries, tossing to coat. Cover and refrigerate for at least 2 hours or until next day.

To serve, spoon berry mixture into serving dishes; top each serving with sour cream, if desired. Makes 6 to 8 servings.

Per serving: .97 gram protein, 35 grams carbohydrates, .56 gram total fat, 0 milligram cholesterol, 4 milligrams sodium.

Berries with Chantilly Custard

Preparation time: 30 to 35 minutes
Chilling time: 2 to 24 hours

Calories per serving: 180

A silky custard sauce, flavored with a dash of almond or orange liqueur, offers the perfect foil for the tart sweetness of summer berries. You can use small strawberries, raspberries, blackberries, or blueberries—or a combination of several types.

>   ½ **cup lowfat milk**
>   1 **piece vanilla bean (3 to 4 inches long), split lengthwise; or ½ teaspoon vanilla**
> 1½ **tablespoons sugar**

>   3 **egg yolks**
>   1 **tablespoon almond- or orange-flavored liqueur**
>   ½ **cup whipping cream**
>   3 **to 4 cups small strawberries (hulled), raspberries, blackberries, or blueberries**

In a 1- to 2-quart pan, scald milk with vanilla bean over medium heat (if using vanilla, add later, as directed). In a small bowl, beat sugar and egg yolks with a wire whisk until blended. Beat about ⅓ of the hot milk into egg mixture, then pour mixture back into pan. Reduce heat to low and cook, stirring, until custard coats the back of a metal spoon in a thin, velvety layer (about 15 minutes); do not allow custard to boil.

Immediately remove from heat and stir until slightly cooled. Stir in vanilla (if used) and liqueur. Cover custard and refrigerate until cold or until next day. Lift out vanilla bean, rinse, let dry, and reserve for reuse.

To serve, in a small bowl, beat cream until it holds stiff peaks; fold into chilled custard. Spoon custard cream into 5 large (about 12-oz.) wine glasses or dessert bowls. Spoon berries equally atop custard cream. Makes 5 servings.

Per serving: 4 grams protein, 15 grams carbohydrates, 12 grams total fat, 192 milligrams cholesterol, 27 milligrams sodium.

Strawberry-filled Melon Bowls

Preparation time: 60 to 70 minutes
Chilling time: 2 to 6 hours

Calories per serving: 269

The cantaloupe is a wonderful choice for a light dessert—not only is it luscious alone, but its natural cavity makes it an ideal "bowl" for fruit and other fillings. These melon halves are cut with a pretty zigzag edge and filled with strawberries in orange syrup.

>   2 **large oranges**
>   1 **cup water**
>   ½ **cup sugar**
>   2 **tablespoons orange-flavored liqueur (optional)**
>   **About 2 cups strawberries**
>   2 **large cantaloupes**

Using a vegetable peeler or a sharp knife, thinly pare peel (orange part only) from oranges; cut peel into thin strips about 1 inch long. Place peel in a small pan and add water; bring to a simmer, then cover and simmer until tender to bite (about 10 minutes). Drain.

Squeeze juice from oranges (you should have about 1 cup). In another small pan, combine orange juice and sugar. Bring to a boil; then reduce heat and boil gently, uncovered, until mixture is reduced to ¾ cup (about 15 minutes). Add drained orange peel and cook for 3 more minutes. Let cool, then stir in liqueur, if desired. Cover and refrigerate until cold.

Hull and slice strawberries; gently stir into cold orange syrup. (At this point, you may cover and refrigerate for up to 4 hours.) To serve, cut cantaloupes in half, making a zigzag or plain edge. Scoop out and discard seeds. Spoon strawberries and syrup equally into melon halves. Makes 4 servings.

Per serving: 4 grams protein, 66 grams carbohydrates, 1 gram total fat, 0 milligram cholesterol, 32 milligrams sodium.

Cantaloupe in Strawberry Purée
· ·

Preparation time: 15 to 25 minutes
Chilling time: 2 hours

Calories per serving: 127

Celebrate two popular summer fruits with this easy, delicious dessert. It's a special way to show off melon and strawberries at the height of their sweetness.

    1 **cup sliced hulled strawberries**
    3 **tablespoons sugar**
    ¼ **cup sweet sherry**
    1 **tablespoon lemon juice**
    1 **large cantaloupe**

In a blender or food processor, whirl strawberries until puréed (you should have ½ cup purée). Pour into a large bowl; stir in sugar, sherry, and lemon juice. Halve cantaloupe; scoop out and discard seeds. Cut off and discard rind; cut fruit into bite-size pieces. Add melon to strawberry purée and stir until evenly coated. Cover and refrigerate for 2 hours to blend flavors.

To serve, spoon fruit and purée equally into 4 large stemmed glasses. Makes 4 servings.

Per serving: 2 grams protein, 27 grams carbohydrates, .61 gram total fat, 0 milligram cholesterol, 17 milligrams sodium.

Spiced Almonds & Melon
· ·

Preparation time: 25 to 30 minutes

Calories per serving: 178

When something sweet would be welcome and time is short, try these juicy melon wedges sprinkled with spiced nuts.

    ½ **cup whole blanched almonds**
    2 **tablespoons sugar**
    ¼ **teaspoon ground nutmeg**
    4 **wedges cantaloupe, Persian, or Crenshaw melon**

Spread almonds in a shallow baking pan; toast in a 350° oven until golden (about 8 minutes), shaking pan occasionally to turn nuts. Let cool completely.

Place almonds, sugar, and nutmeg in a blender or food processor. Whirl until almonds are finely ground. Place 1 melon wedge on each of 4 individual plates; sprinkle almond mixture evenly over melon. Makes 4 servings.

Per serving: 5 grams protein, 21 grams carbohydrates, 10 grams total fat, 0 milligram cholesterol, 14 milligrams sodium.

Minted Melon Balls
· ·

Preparation time: 20 to 30 minutes
Chilling time: about 1 hour

Calories per serving: 92

A combination of melon balls—cantaloupe, watermelon, honeydew, Crenshaw, and Persian—makes a colorful dessert to show off in a clear glass salad bowl.

    1½ **tablespoons coarsely chopped fresh mint or 2 teaspoons crumbled dry mint**
    ⅓ **cup sugar**
    ½ **cup water**
    2 **tablespoons orange juice**
    1 **tablespoon lemon juice**
    8 **cups assorted melon balls or bite-size pieces (see suggestions in recipe introduction)**
       Mint sprigs (optional)

Place chopped mint in a small bowl; set aside.

Combine sugar and water in a small pan; bring to a boil over high heat, stirring until sugar is dissolved. Continue to boil, uncovered, for 5 minutes. Pour over mint, cover, and refrigerate for about 1 hour. Pour syrup through a wire strainer and discard mint. Stir in orange juice and lemon juice; cover and refrigerate until cold.

To serve, pile melon balls in a serving bowl, arranging them in layers, if desired. Pour chilled syrup over melon and garnish with mint sprigs, if desired. Makes 6 to 8 servings.

Per serving: 1 gram protein, 23 grams carbohydrates, .30 gram total fat, 0 milligram cholesterol, 16 milligrams sodium.

Dramatic in its simplicity, Peaches in Almond Cream (recipe on facing page)
showcases ripe summer peaches. A velvety almond sauce
brings out the perfumy flavor of the pitted, sliced fruit.

· ·

Peaches in Almond Cream

(Pictured on facing page)
Preparation time: 20 to 30 minutes

Calories per serving: 224

Peaches and cream: a culinary cliché? Perhaps, but they go together so well that it would be hard to tire of the combination. This interpretation of the classic duo finds fresh peach slices arranged in a pool of almond cream sauce for a simple yet stunning dessert.

About 1 tablespoon sliced almonds
1 cup sour cream
3 tablespoons firmly packed brown sugar
1 tablespoon almond-flavored liqueur or ⅛ teaspoon almond extract
2 or 3 large ripe peaches
4 small mint sprigs

Spread almonds in a shallow baking pan and toast in a 350° oven until golden (about 8 minutes), stirring frequently. Set aside.

In a small bowl, beat sour cream, sugar, and liqueur until smooth. Divide sour cream sauce equally among 4 salad or dessert plates, spreading it into a circle on each.

Peel peaches, if desired; then pit and slice. Arrange an equal portion of peach slices in cream on each plate. Garnish each serving with ¼ of the toasted almond slices and a mint sprig. Makes 4 servings.

Per serving: 3 grams protein, 26 grams carbohydrates, 13 grams total fat, 25 milligrams cholesterol, 34 milligrams sodium.

Spiced Peaches in Wine

Preparation time: 10 to 15 minutes
Standing time: 2 to 8 hours

Calories per serving: 42

Summer is prime time for big, beautiful, juicy peaches. Try soaking them in a spiced wine syrup for an easy dessert that lets the natural fruit flavor shine through.

½ cup burgundy
2 tablespoons powdered sugar
1 cinnamon stick (about 3 inches long)
1 teaspoon lemon juice
Peel cut from ½ lemon (yellow part only)
3 ripe peaches, peeled, halved, and pitted

In a small pan, combine burgundy, sugar, cinnamon stick, lemon juice, and lemon peel. Bring to a boil over high heat; then reduce heat and simmer, uncovered, for 3 minutes.

Place peaches in a serving bowl; pour hot syrup over them and turn fruit to coat. Let stand at room temperature for at least 2 hours or up to 8 hours (refrigerate to keep longer). Serve at room temperature. Makes 3 to 6 servings.

Per serving: .47 gram protein, 11 grams carbohydrates, .06 gram total fat, 0 milligram cholesterol, 1 milligram sodium.

Peach Brûlée

Preparation time: 25 to 30 minutes
Broiling time: about 2 minutes

Calories per serving: 131

Simple embellishments can turn fresh fruits into interesting desserts without obscuring their natural character. Consider, for example, this tempting combination of peaches and blueberries with a caramelized crust of brown sugar.

2 tablespoons butter or margarine, melted
2 tablespoons lemon juice
3 large peaches, peeled, halved, and pitted
½ cup blueberries
Nonstick cooking spray
6 tablespoons firmly packed brown sugar
Mint sprigs

In a shallow bowl, mix butter and lemon juice. Turn peach halves in butter mixture to coat; then arrange, cut side up, in a large broiler pan. Fill each peach cavity with 1 tablespoon of the blueberries. Set aside.

Line a large baking sheet with foil and generously coat with cooking spray. Push 1 tablespoon of the sugar through a sieve onto foil to make an even layer about 3 inches square; repeat with remaining 5 tablespoons sugar, making a total of 6 squares. Broil about 6 inches below heat until sugar is melted (1 to 2 minutes); watch carefully to avoid scorching. Let cool until set but still pliable (about 30 seconds).

With a wide spatula, set a sugar square atop each peach half.

Broil about 6 inches below heat just until sugar crust drapes around peach (10 to 30 seconds). Transfer each peach half to a small bowl. Garnish servings with mint and remaining 2 tablespoons blueberries. Serve immediately. Makes 6 servings.

Per serving: .71 gram protein, 24 grams carbohydrates, 4 grams total fat, 10 milligrams cholesterol, 45 milligrams sodium.

A bowl of seasonal fresh fruit or a scoop of frozen yogurt makes a perfectly delicious light dessert all on its own, but there are times when you want a bit of embellishment. Here are some ideas.

Our Wine & Berry Compote, Currant or Gooseberry Relish, and all four fruit sauces are good over your favorite creamy frozen dessert—whether ice milk, yogurt, or sherbet. Gjetost-Yogurt Dressing, made from curiously sweet Norwegian gjetost cheese, is a high-protein sauce that tastes great with fresh fruit. Whipped Topping, made with dry milk, is our low-calorie substitute for whipped cream. And caramel-nut–flavored Praline Powder makes an elegant crowning touch for both fruit and frozen desserts.

Spirited Cranberry-Orange Sauce

2 packages (12 oz. *each*) fresh cranberries (6 cups *total*)
1½ cups sugar
1 cup orange juice
¾ cup orange-flavored liqueur
4 large oranges

In a 4- to 5-quart pan, combine cranberries, sugar, orange juice, and liqueur. Bring to a boil over high heat; then reduce heat to medium and boil gently, stirring often, until berries soften and sauce begins to thicken slightly (8 to 10 minutes). Let cool. (At this point, you may cover and refrigerate for up to 3 days. Freeze for longer storage; thaw before continuing.)

To serve, cut peel and all white membrane from oranges with a sharp knife. Hold oranges over pan of cranberry sauce to catch juice; cut segments free, lift out, and add to sauce. Stir gently to blend. Serve cool. Makes about 6 cups.

Apricot or Plum Sauce

1½ pounds firm-ripe or fully ripe apricots or plums
½ cup water
½ to 1 cup sugar

Cut apricots in halves or quarters; discard pits. (Or cut plums away from pits; discard pits.)

In a 2- to 3-quart pan, combine fruit and water. Bring to a boil; then reduce heat, cover, and simmer until fruit begins to soften (3 to 5 minutes). If needed, add more water to give sauce the consistency desired. Stir in sugar, adjusting amount to taste. Continue to simmer until fruit falls apart to make a sauce (2 to 5 more minutes). Serve warm or chilled. To store, cover and refrigerate for up to 2 days. Makes 3 or 4 servings.

Raspberry or Strawberry Sauce

1 package (10 oz.) frozen sweetened raspberries or strawberries, thawed
½ teaspoon cornstarch
1 tablespoon light corn syrup

In a small pan, combine raspberries and their juice, cornstarch, and corn syrup. Bring to a full boil over medium-high heat; continue to boil, uncovered, stirring constantly, for 2 minutes. Let cool, then cover and refrigerate (sauce thickens as it chills). Serve chilled. Makes about 1 cup.

Blueberry Sauce

(Pictured on page 78)

⅓ cup sugar
1 tablespoon cornstarch
2 cups fresh blueberries; or 2 cups frozen unsweetened blueberries, thawed and drained
2 tablespoons lemon juice
⅓ cup water

In a small pan, mix sugar and cornstarch. Stir in blueberries, lemon juice, and water. Cook over medium heat, stirring, until sauce is thickened. Serve warm or chilled. Makes about 2 cups.

Gjetost-Yogurt Dressing

1 cup (4 oz.) shredded gjetost cheese
2 tablespoons firmly packed brown sugar
1 cup plain lowfat yogurt

In a blender or food processor, whirl cheese, sugar, and ½ cup of the yogurt until smooth; scrape down sides of container with a rubber spatula as needed.

Gently stir together cheese mixture and remaining ½ cup yogurt just until blended. Cover and refrigerate for at least 1 hour or up to 1 week. To serve, spoon dressing over fresh fruit. Makes about 1½ cups dressing; allow 2 to 4 tablespoons for a 1-cup serving of fruit.

Praline Powder

2 cups sugar
1 cup hazelnuts (filberts) or whole unblanched almonds

Pour sugar into a 10- to 12-inch frying pan; spread to make an even layer. Set over medium heat and let stand undisturbed until sugar begins to melt. With a wooden spoon, push melted portion to edges, allowing unmelted sugar to come to center. When almost all sugar has melted, add hazelnuts. Push mixture in pan from side to side until sugar is completely melted and a light caramel color (this happens quickly). Remove from heat immediately; pour onto a large (at least 12 by 15 inches), well-buttered sheet of foil. Let cool until hard (at least 30 minutes).

Break into chunks no larger than 2 inches square (1 inch square if using blender to grind into powder). Place about ¼ of the chunks at a time in a food processor or blender; process until granules are the size of rock salt. Store powder in an airtight container at room temperature for up to 6 months. Makes 3 cups.

Whipped Topping

1 envelope unflavored gelatin
4 teaspoons cold water
⅓ cup boiling water
1 cup ice water
1⅓ cups instant nonfat dry milk powder
6 tablespoons sugar
⅓ cup salad oil
1 teaspoon vanilla
2 teaspoons lemon juice

Refrigerate beaters and large bowl of an electric mixer until very cold. In a cup, sprinkle gelatin over the 4 teaspoons cold water; let stand for about 5 minutes to soften. Then add boiling water and stir until gelatin is completely dissolved. Let cool to room temperature (if mixture sets before you're ready to use it, set cup in hot water to soften gelatin again).

In chilled mixer bowl, combine ice water and dry milk. Beat on high speed until mixture holds soft peaks (about 5 minutes); if mixture spatters, drape a towel or wax paper loosely over bowl and beaters. Gradually add sugar, beating constantly. Scrape down bowl sides, then continue to beat, gradually pouring in oil, vanilla, lemon juice, and gelatin mixture. Scrape down bowl sides; beat for 1 more minute. Transfer to a rigid container, cover airtight, and refrigerate or freeze. Makes about 6 cups.

Wine & Berry Compote

1 cup *each* dry red wine and water
¾ cup sugar
6 tablespoons lemon juice
1 vanilla bean (6 to 7 inches long), split lengthwise; or 1 teaspoon vanilla
1 to 1½ pounds (4 to 6 cups) mixed berries, such as strawberries (hulled), raspberries, blackberries or blueberries

In a 4- to 5-quart pan, combine wine, water, sugar, lemon juice, and vanilla bean (if using vanilla, add later, as directed). Bring to a boil over high heat, stirring until

sugar is dissolved; continue to boil, uncovered, until syrup is reduced to 1¼ cups. Stir in vanilla (if used).

Lift out vanilla bean and scrape seeds into syrup; rinse bean, let dry, and reserve for reuse. (At this point, you may let syrup cool, then cover and refrigerate for up to 3 weeks. Bring to a simmer before continuing.)

Gently stir berries into hot syrup; set aside until slightly cooled, then serve. Makes 6 to 8 servings.

Currant or Gooseberry Relish

½ cup water
⅓ cup *each* sugar and orange juice
1½ tablespoons lemon juice
¾ cup red currants (stemmed) or gooseberries (blossom ends removed)
½ teaspoon finely shredded orange peel

In a 1- to 1½-quart pan, combine water, sugar, orange juice, and lemon juice; bring to a boil over high heat, stirring until sugar is dissolved. Reduce heat to medium. Add ½ cup of the currants and bring to a boil; continue to boil, uncovered, until reduced to 1 cup (about 30 minutes).

Add remaining ¼ cup currants and continue to cook just until some of them begin to pop (about 3 minutes). Stir in orange peel. Serve relish warm or cool. If made ahead, cover cooled relish and refrigerate for up to 2 days; reheat before serving, if desired. Makes 1 to 1¼ cups; allow 2 to 4 tablespoons for a serving.

Peaches with Almond Crust

Preparation time: 30 to 40 minutes
Baking time: 30 to 35 minutes

Calories per serving: 165

Something like a cobbler, something like a soufflé, this peachy creation is a true original. You pour a ground-almond batter over peeled peach halves and bake until golden brown, then serve warm.

> ¾ cup whole unblanched almonds
> 5 medium-size firm-ripe peaches
> 2 eggs
> ⅓ cup sugar
> ¼ teaspoon almond extract
> 1½ cups Whipped Topping (page 41) or whipped cream

Spread almonds in a shallow baking pan and toast in a 350° oven until light golden beneath skins (about 8 minutes), shaking pan occasionally to turn nuts. Let cool, then whirl in a blender or food processor until finely ground. Increase oven temperature to 375°.

Peel, halve, and pit peaches. Set peach halves, cut side down, in a buttered shallow 1½-quart baking dish. In small bowl of an electric mixer, beat eggs, sugar, and almond extract until thick and lemon-colored; mix in almonds. Pour batter over fruit and bake, uncovered, in a 375° oven until golden brown (30 to 35 minutes). Serve warm, with Whipped Topping. Makes 10 servings.

Per serving: 5 grams protein, 19 grams carbohydrates, 9 grams total fat, 55 milligrams cholesterol, 28 milligrams sodium.

Peach Betty

Preparation time: 25 to 35 minutes
Baking time: about 55 minutes

Calories per serving: 226

Apple Betty is an old-fashioned dessert that many of us remember from childhood. Enjoy it again today, with these delicious changes: use peaches or pears instead of apples, and try whole wheat bread for extra flavor and wholesomeness.

> 3 cups cubed stale whole wheat bread
> ⅓ cup butter or margarine, melted
> 6 cups peeled, thinly sliced ripe peaches, pears, or apples
> 1 cup firmly packed brown sugar
> 2 tablespoons lemon juice

> ½ teaspoon grated lemon peel
> 1 teaspoon *each* ground cinnamon and vanilla
> ½ teaspoon ground nutmeg
> ½ cup raisins
> ¾ cup hot water
> ½ cup chopped nuts

Toss together bread cubes and butter; set aside. In a large bowl, mix peaches, sugar, lemon juice, lemon peel, cinnamon, vanilla, nutmeg, and raisins.

Spread ⅓ of the buttered bread cubes in a buttered 2-quart casserole with a lid; top with half the peach mixture, then half the remaining bread cubes. Evenly layer on remaining peach mixture and remaining bread cubes. Pour hot water over all.

Cover and bake in a 350° oven for 45 minutes. Uncover, sprinkle with nuts, and continue to bake until top is well browned (about 10 more minutes). Serve warm. Makes 12 servings.

Per serving: 3 grams protein, 38 grams carbohydrates, 9 grams total fat, 14 milligrams cholesterol, 109 milligrams sodium.

Minted Poached Pears

(Pictured on facing page)
Preparation time: 10 to 15 minutes
Cooking time: 30 to 45 minutes

Calories per serving: 204

There's more than one way to poach a pear. These are cooked in unsweetened pineapple juice, boiled down to intensify its flavor and enlivened with a dash of crème de menthe.

> 2 cans (12 oz. *each*) unsweetened pineapple juice
> 4 small or medium-size firm-ripe pears (such as d'Anjou, Bosc, or Winter Nellis)
> 2 tablespoons crème de menthe or ¼ teaspoon mint extract
> Mint sprigs

Pour juice into a 3-quart pan and set over medium heat. Peel pears, leaving stems in place; remove core of each pear by inserting an apple corer through blossom end. Place pears in juice; when juice comes to a boil, reduce heat, cover, and simmer until pears are just tender when pierced (10 to 25 minutes).

With a slotted spoon, lift pears from juice and place in a serving dish. Boil juice over high heat, uncovered, stirring often, until reduced to 1 to 1⅓ cups. Stir in crème de menthe. Pour syrup over pears; if desired, cover and refrigerate until cold. Garnish with mint before serving. Makes 4 servings.

Per serving: 1 gram protein, 47 grams carbohydrates, .64 gram total fat, 0 milligram cholesterol, 2 milligrams sodium.

Fresh pears are natural beauties, requiring no fancy embellishments to make a smashing
dessert. Minted Poached Pears (recipe on facing page) are simply cooked
in unsweetened pineapple juice lightly accented with crème de menthe.

• •

Wine-poached Pears

Preparation time: about 10 minutes
Cooking time: 25 to 35 minutes

Calories per serving: 99

Two kinds of wine flavor these easy-to-make poached pears. One is a dry red, the other a sweet white wine such as Muscat Canelli or late-harvest Riesling.

- 4 to 6 small firm-ripe Bartlett pears
- 2 cups Muscat Canelli or late-harvest sweet Johannisberg Riesling
- 2 cups dry red wine

Peel pears; leave stems in place. If desired, remove core of each pear by inserting an apple corer through blossom end. Lay pears side by side in a 5- to 6-quart pan. Add Muscat Canelli and red wine; turn pears over to coat evenly. Bring to a boil; then reduce heat, cover, and simmer until pears are just tender when pierced (10 to 20 minutes).

Lift out pears, arrange in a shallow serving dish, and set aside. Increase heat to high and boil until wine mixture is reduced to about ⅔ cup; pour over pears. If made ahead, let stand at room temperature for up to 4 hours or cover and refrigerate until next day, basting pears several times with wine mixture.

To serve, place 1 pear in each of 4 to 6 individual dessert glasses. Spoon wine mixture evenly over top. Makes 4 to 6 servings.

Per serving: .62 gram protein, 25 grams carbohydrates, .49 gram total fat, 0 milligram cholesterol, 8 milligrams sodium.

Meringue-topped Pears

Preparation time: 40 to 50 minutes
Baking time: 45 to 50 minutes

Calories per serving: 128

For a company dessert that's not too rich, consider oven-poached pear halves topped with airy puffs of meringue. Crystallized ginger, lemon peel, and sherry flavor the fruit.

- 4 large firm-ripe pears, peeled, halved, and cored
- ¼ cup granulated sugar
- 1 teaspoon grated lemon peel
- 4 teaspoons chopped crystallized ginger
- ¼ cup sweet sherry or apple juice
- 2 egg whites
- ⅛ teaspoon *each* salt and cream of tartar
- ¼ cup firmly packed brown sugar
- ½ teaspoon vanilla

Place pear halves, cut side up and slightly apart, in a 7- by 11-inch baking dish. Stir together granulated sugar, lemon peel, and ginger; press equal portions into each pear cavity. Pour sherry around pears in baking dish, cover, and bake in a 350° oven until pears are tender when pierced (about 40 minutes). Remove pears from oven and set aside. Increase oven temperature to 400°.

Combine egg whites, salt, and cream of tartar in small bowl of an electric mixer; beat until whites hold soft peaks. Gradually add brown sugar and continue to beat until mixture holds stiff peaks. Beat in vanilla.

Top pears evenly with meringue. Bake, uncovered, until meringue is golden brown (about 8 minutes). Serve warm; or let cool slightly, then refrigerate and serve cold. Makes 8 servings.

Per serving: 1 gram protein, 32 grams carbohydrates, .41 gram total fat, 0 milligram cholesterol, 51 milligrams sodium.

Baked Cinnamon Pears

Preparation time: 20 to 25 minutes
Baking time: 35 to 45 minutes

Calories per serving: 289

On a chilly winter's evening, these warm baked pears make a satisfying dessert. Flavored with cinnamon, nutmeg, and raisins, they're also an appealing choice for breakfast or brunch.

- 6 medium-size firm-ripe pears
- 1½ tablespoons lemon juice
- 5 tablespoons butter or margarine, softened
- ½ cup *each* firmly packed brown sugar and raisins
- ½ teaspoon ground cinnamon
- ¼ teaspoon ground nutmeg
- ¼ cup water

Core pears by inserting an apple corer through blossom end. Cut a ½-inch-wide strip of peel from stem end of each pear. Set pears upright and slightly apart in a shallow 9- to 11-inch round or square baking dish. Sprinkle with lemon juice.

In a small bowl, mix butter, sugar, raisins, cinnamon, and nutmeg. Divide mixture evenly among pear centers, packing in lightly. Distribute any remaining mixture in chunks over bottom of baking dish. Pour water around pears; cover dish tightly with foil and bake in a 400° oven until pears are tender when pierced (35 to 45 minutes). Serve warm. Makes 6 servings.

Per serving: 1 gram protein, 53 grams carbohydrates, 10 grams total fat, 26 milligrams cholesterol, 105 milligrams sodium.

Pear Fans with Orange Syrup

(Pictured on page 3)
Preparation time: 20 to 30 minutes

Calories per serving: 192

Designed to show off the rosy color of red pears, this dessert is simple and elegant. If red pears are not available in your market, you can use yellow ones.

- ½ cup *each* sugar and orange juice
- ¼ cup butter or margarine
- 2 tablespoons lemon juice
- 1 teaspoon finely shredded orange or lemon peel
- 3 medium-size red or yellow pears
  Shredded orange or lemon peel (optional)

In a 2- to 3-quart pan, combine sugar, orange juice, butter, and 1 tablespoon of the lemon juice; stir over high heat until butter is melted. Remove from heat; stir in the 1 teaspoon orange peel. (At this point, you may cover and refrigerate for up to 1 day.)

Cut pears in half lengthwise. Trim core, stem end, and blossom end from each half; rub cut surfaces with some of the remaining 1 tablespoon lemon juice to prevent darkening. Then slice each pear half lengthwise into ¼-inch strips, leaving stem end intact; cut from rounded end to within about ½ inch of stem end (see photo on page 3). Drizzle cuts with remaining lemon juice.

Place each pear half, cut side down, on a dessert plate. With the palm of your hand, lightly press cut portion down and away from you to fan out slices. Reheat orange syrup to simmering; spoon over fruit, dividing equally. Garnish with orange peel, if desired. Makes 6 servings.

Per serving: .56 gram protein, 32 grams carbohydrates, 8 grams total fat, 21 milligrams cholesterol, 79 milligrams sodium.

Pear-Blueberry Crisp

Preparation time: 20 to 30 minutes
Baking time: about 45 minutes

Calories per serving: 293

Blueberries are delectable—but often costly. Make the most of a small amount by combining them with juicy pear chunks, then baking the fruit under a nutty streusel topping.

- 2 cups fresh blueberries; or 2 cups frozen unsweetened blueberries, thawed and drained
- 4 medium-size ripe pears, peeled, cored, and sliced
- ¼ cup granulated sugar
- 2 tablespoons *each* lemon juice and water
- ¼ cup firmly packed brown sugar
- 1 cup rolled oats
- ½ cup chopped walnuts
- ⅓ cup all-purpose flour
- ⅓ cup firm butter or margarine
  Vanilla Frozen Yogurt (page 72), Whipped Topping (page 41), or whipped cream (optional)

In a shallow 1½-quart baking dish, combine blueberries, pears, granulated sugar, lemon juice, and water; stir to mix evenly.

In a small bowl, combine brown sugar, rolled oats, walnuts, and flour. Cut butter into pieces, add to flour mixture, and rub between your fingers until mixture resembles coarse crumbs. Sprinkle evenly over fruit.

Bake, uncovered, in a 350° oven until topping is richly browned and pears are tender when pierced (about 45 minutes). Serve hot or cooled. To serve, spoon into bowls; top individual servings with yogurt, if desired. Makes 8 servings.

Per serving: 4 grams protein, 43 grams carbohydrates, 13 grams total fat, 20 milligrams cholesterol, 84 milligrams sodium.

Glazed Pears

Preparation time: 5 to 10 minutes
Cooking time: 10 to 15 minutes

Calories per serving: 169

Thickly sliced pears are simmered in a cinnamon syrup to make this simple dessert. Crisp plain cookies would be a nice accompaniment for the fruit. To prevent the pear slices from darkening, cut them just before cooking.

- 3 large ripe pears, peeled if desired
- 2 tablespoons butter or margarine
- 2 tablespoons firmly packed brown sugar
- ¾ teaspoon ground cinnamon

Core pears by inserting an apple corer through blossom end; cut crosswise into 1-inch-thick rings. Melt butter in a wide frying pan over medium heat. Add sugar and cinnamon; stir until sugar is dissolved. Add pears and cook, turning gently with a wide spatula, until just tender when pierced (7 to 10 minutes). Serve warm. Makes 4 servings.

Per serving: .67 gram protein, 30 grams carbohydrates, 6 grams total fat, 16 milligrams cholesterol, 61 milligrams sodium.

Frosty fun on a stick—that's the way to describe Frozen Yogurt Bananas (recipe on page 28).
Coated with yogurt and rolled in toasted coconut
or almonds, they make an informal dessert for a family supper.

. . . .

Brandied Ricotta with Fruit

Preparation time: 15 to 20 minutes
Chilling time: at least 3 hours

Calories per serving: 229

Here's a "help-yourself" dessert that your guests will enjoy. Spoon a mound of sweetened ricotta cheese, flavored with brandy and cinnamon, on a serving plate; surround the cheese with fresh fruit and plain cookies. Diners spread the cheese mixture on their choice of fruit and cookies, or make open-faced cookie "sandwiches."

- 1 **pound (2 cups) ricotta cheese**
- ¼ **cup powdered sugar**
- 2 **tablespoons brandy**
- ¼ **teaspoon ground cinnamon**
- 8 **plums or small peaches; or 24 large strawberries**
- 24 **mildly sweet cookies (such as petit beurre)**

In small bowl of an electric mixer, beat together ricotta cheese, sugar, brandy, and cinnamon until smooth. Mound cheese mixture on a serving plate and swirl in a cone shape; cover lightly and refrigerate for several hours.

To serve, halve and pit plums or peaches (leave strawberries whole and unhulled); arrange fruit around cheese. Set cookies on another plate; serve alongside cheese and fruit. To eat, spread cheese on fruit and cookies. Makes 8 servings.

Per serving: 8 grams protein, 28 grams carbohydrates, 9 grams total fat, 22 milligrams cholesterol, 128 milligrams sodium.

Poached Prune Plums

Preparation time: about 10 minutes
Cooking time: 10 to 15 minutes

Calories per serving: 168

Good warm or chilled, these purple plums are briefly cooked in a syrup spiced with cinnamon, ginger, cloves, and nutmeg. They're delicious plain or topped with sour cream; you might also serve the fruit over cake for a plum shortcake.

- **About 1½ pounds prune plums**
- ¾ **cup sugar**
- ½ **teaspoon pumpkin pie spice; or ⅛ teaspoon *each* ground cinnamon, ginger, cloves, and nutmeg**
- 2 **tablespoons orange juice**
- 4 **teaspoons lemon juice**

Dash of salt
2 **tablespoons *each* cornstarch and water, stirred together**
Sour cream (optional)

Halve and pit plums; you should have about 3 cups. Place plums in a 2-quart pan and add sugar, pumpkin pie spice, orange juice, lemon juice, and salt. Bring to a boil over high heat; then reduce heat, cover, and simmer until plums are just tender when pierced (6 to 8 minutes). Stir in cornstarch mixture; cook, stirring, until clear and thickened.

Serve warm or chilled. To serve, spoon plums and juices into dessert bowls; offer sour cream to spoon over fruit, if desired. Makes 4 to 6 servings.

Per serving: .88 gram protein, 42 grams carbohydrates, .67 gram total fat, 0 milligram cholesterol, 23 milligrams sodium.

Red Grapes with Sherried Cream

Preparation time: 25 to 35 minutes
Chilling time: at least 3 hours

Calories per serving: 252

To make this elegant dessert, simply layer spoonfuls of sherry-flavored custard and plump seedless red grapes in stemmed glasses.

- ⅓ **cup sugar**
- 2 **tablespoons cornstarch**
- ⅛ **teaspoon salt**
- 2 **cups lowfat milk**
- ¼ **cup sweet sherry or apple juice**
- 2 **egg yolks**
- 2 **tablespoons butter or margarine**
- 1 **teaspoon vanilla**
- **About 1½ cups seedless red grapes**

In a 2-quart pan, stir together sugar, cornstarch, and salt. Gradually add milk and sherry, stirring until well blended. Bring to a boil over medium heat, stirring constantly; continue to boil, uncovered, for 1 minute. Remove from heat.

In a small bowl, lightly beat egg yolks. Stir a little of the hot sauce into beaten yolks, then pour yolk mixture into pan and cook over medium heat, stirring, for 30 seconds. Remove from heat; add butter and vanilla and stir until butter is melted.

Layer spoonfuls of pudding and grapes in 4 stemmed glasses. Cover and refrigerate until cold before serving. Makes 4 servings.

Per serving: 6 grams protein, 33 grams carbohydrates, 11 grams total fat, 161 milligrams cholesterol, 194 milligrams sodium.

Fruit on a stick, fruit in an icy bath, fruit with yogurt and honey—these are simple ways in which the fresh harvest of the season is presented in other countries. They're well worth investigating if you seek easily prepared, good-looking refreshments for warm summer days.

Fruit on a Stick

In Guadalajara, street vendors offer a colorful array of fruit on wooden sticks. You might serve such skewered fruit as dessert on the patio, or as an accompaniment for bubbly champagne or wine punch at an afternoon party. In any case, you'll probably want to serve the fruit outdoors, since it tends to drip as you munch.

How to Prepare

To hold pieces of fruit, you can use sturdy plastic forks, pointed wooden chopsticks, blunt wooden chopsticks with narrow ends sharpened in a pencil sharpener, or ¼-inch dowels cut to various lengths and sharpened.

To support the holders, force them into a slab of styrene foam about 1½ inches thick. Conceal the foam with greenery, such as ivy, citrus leaves, or parsley.

Fruits suitable for serving on a stick (sturdy enough to stay in place and not apt to discolor) include small mangoes, nectarines, small oranges, papayas, pineapple, large strawberries, and the melons—casaba, cantaloupe, Crenshaw, honeydew, Persian, and watermelon.

To prepare fruit: peel mangoes, leaving a section of skin at base; then gash fruit to the pit in several places and press flesh away from pit. (This gives the mango a flower-like look and makes it easier to eat.) Cut nectarines in halves and remove pits. Cut unpeeled oranges into quarters. Peel papayas, then cut lengthwise in halves or quarters; scoop out and discard seeds. Cut peel from pineapple; cut fruit into slices or half slices. Hull strawberries. Cut rind from all melons, then cut fruit into slices or chunks.

For a surprise addition to the selection, include cucumbers (a popular choice in Mexico). Cut them into 2- to 3-inch lengths, then crosshatch 1 end about 1 inch deep.

Gently secure fruit on forks or sticks and set firmly into the styrene foam. To keep the fruit looking fresh, spray it occasionally with a fine mist of water. Have a container available for discarding used sticks.

Bathed Fruits

For an extra-simple presentation, try serving fruits in a bowl of ice water—a practice common in Italian restaurants. The water chills the fruit just enough to make it refreshing without dulling the flavor, and rinses away any flecks of dust. A centerpiece of sun-warmed fruit picked from your own garden would benefit from this quick, chilly bath.

How to Prepare

Fruits enhanced by a brief immersion in ice water just before serving include apples, apricots, cherries, figs, grapes, nectarines, peaches, pears, and plums. Put a selection of fruit in a pretty glass bowl filled with ice and water, then pass it around. Or fill one bowl with ice and water, another with fruit; let guests serve themselves, dipping their choice of fruit in the cold bath.

Milk Bar Fruits

Another summer fruit idea comes from Belgian "milk bars." Fresh berries or other fruits are spooned onto plain yogurt, whipped cream, or sour cream, then drizzled with honey. The combination is delicious for dessert and equally appealing for brunch.

Choose your favorite brand of plain yogurt, or use our Thick Homemade Yogurt (page 61).

How to Prepare

Allow at least ½ cup yogurt (or unsweetened whipped cream or sour cream) per serving. Place all the yogurt in a serving bowl nested in a larger bowl of ice to keep it very cold.

Surround yogurt with dishes of at least 3 of the following: hulled strawberries, blueberries, raspberries, or other berries; dark sweet cherries (leave stems on to use as "handles" for eating, if desired; or stem and pit cherries); and sliced plums, nectarines, or peaches (sprinkle with lemon juice to prevent darkening). Allow a total of ½ to ¾ cup fruit per person.

Accompany fruit and yogurt with a small pitcher of honey. Each person ladles some yogurt into a bowl, adds fruit, drizzles the combination with honey, and eats with a spoon.

Mixed Grape Compote

Preparation time: 25 to 35 minutes
Chilling time: at least 3 hours

Calories per serving: 150

Red, green, and black seedless grapes, gently poached in champagne syrup, make a festive and colorful conclusion to a summer meal.

- ¾ cup natural to extra-dry champagne or other sparkling white wine
- ¾ cup water
- ⅔ cup sugar
- 5 tablespoons lemon juice
- 1 vanilla bean (about 7 inches long), split lengthwise; or 1 teaspoon vanilla
- 1 cup *each* seedless green, red, and black grapes (about 1 lb. *total*); or use all 1 color
  Chilled natural to extra-dry champagne or other sparkling white wine

In a 4- to 5-quart pan, combine the ¾ cup champagne, water, sugar, lemon juice, and vanilla bean (if using vanilla, add later, as directed). Bring to a boil over high heat, stirring until sugar is dissolved; continue to boil, uncovered, until reduced to 1 cup. Remove from heat; stir in vanilla, if used.

Lift out vanilla bean and scrape seeds into syrup; rinse bean, let dry, and reserve for reuse. (At this point, you may let syrup cool, then cover and refrigerate for up to 1 week.)

Combine syrup and grapes in a 2- to 3-quart pan. Bring to a boil over high heat; continue to boil, uncovered, just until grapes soften and skins barely begin to burst (about 3 minutes). Let cool, then cover and refrigerate for at least 3 hours or until next day.

To serve, spoon grapes and champagne syrup into 6 champagne glasses. Splash in additional champagne, filling glasses close to brim. Makes 6 servings.

Per serving: .56 gram protein, 38 grams carbohydrates, .46 gram total fat, 0 milligram cholesterol, 6 milligrams sodium.

Fresh Fig & Ricotta Tulips

Preparation time: 25 to 35 minutes

Calories per serving: 192

Take advantage of both the flavor and shape of fresh figs with this attractive light dessert. You cut the figs so they resemble tulips, then spoon a lemony ricotta cheese filling into the center of the "petals." Whole almonds add a crowning touch.

- 12 medium-size to large ripe figs
- 8 ounces (1 cup) ricotta cheese
- ½ teaspoon grated lemon peel
- ⅛ teaspoon salt
- ¾ teaspoon vanilla
- ¼ cup sugar
- 1 egg white
- 12 whole unblanched almonds

Trim stems from figs. Then cut each fig open into a tulip shape by slicing into quarters from stem end to about ½ inch from blossom end. Set aside.

In small bowl of an electric mixer, beat ricotta cheese, lemon peel, salt, vanilla, and 2 tablespoons of the sugar until smoothly blended. In another small bowl, beat egg white until very frothy; gradually add remaining 2 tablespoons sugar and continue to beat until mixture holds stiff peaks. Gently fold into ricotta mixture. (At this point, you may cover and refrigerate figs and ricotta mixture separately for up to 4 hours.)

To serve, arrange 2 or 3 sliced figs upright on each dessert plate. Gently open each fig and spoon about 2 tablespoons of the cheese mixture into center; top with an almond. Makes 4 to 6 servings.

Per serving: 7 grams protein, 31 grams carbohydrates, 6 grams total fat, 12 milligrams cholesterol, 103 milligrams sodium.

Papaya Snow

Preparation time: about 10 minutes
Freezing time: 3 to 4 hours

Calories per serving: 42

Tropical papayas are best when served simply, so their delicate flavor and fragrance can come through. In this recipe, partially frozen papaya is shredded and served with a squeeze of lime. It's an unusual, elegant presentation—and very low in calories.

- 1 large ripe papaya, peeled, halved, and seeded
- 4 lime wedges

Wrap each papaya half in plastic wrap and freeze until solid (3 to 4 hours). Forty-five minutes to 1 hour before serving, remove papaya from freezer and let stand in refrigerator. Just before serving, unwrap each half and shred coarsely. Spoon shredded papaya equally into 4 chilled dessert glasses. Serve immediately; accompany each serving with a lime wedge to squeeze over fruit. Makes 4 servings.

Per serving: .65 gram protein, 11 grams carbohydrates, .14 gram total fat, 0 milligram cholesterol, 3 milligrams sodium.

Papaya Parfaits

Preparation time: about 20 minutes
Chilling time: about 2 hours

Calories per serving: 233

Puréed papaya with a touch of lime is the low-calorie sauce for this tropical treat. You line dessert bowls with fruit, add a scoop of frozen yogurt, and top it all with the naturally sweet papaya sauce.

- 1 large ripe papaya
- 2 tablespoons lime juice
- ½ teaspoon grated lime peel
- 3 cups sliced bananas, fresh orange segments, drained canned mandarin orange segments, papaya slices, or fresh or drained canned pineapple chunks
- 6 scoops (about ½ cup *each*) Vanilla Frozen Yogurt (page 72), purchased frozen yogurt, or orange sherbet

Peel, halve, and seed papaya. Cut fruit into chunks and place in a blender or food processor along with lime juice and lime peel. Whirl until smoothly puréed. Cover and refrigerate until cold.

Line each of 6 individual dessert bowls with ½ cup of the bananas. Top each with 1 scoop of the yogurt; pour chilled papaya mixture equally over yogurt. Makes 6 servings.

Per serving: 7 grams protein, 46 grams carbohydrates, 3 grams total fat, 61 milligrams cholesterol, 72 milligrams sodium.

Papaya with Coconut Dip

Preparation time: 25 to 30 minutes
Chilling time: at least 1 hour

Calories per serving: 222

For a casual dessert that resembles fondue, spear chunks of ripe papaya with a fork, then dip into sour cream sauce and toasted coconut.

- 1 cup sweetened shredded coconut
- 1 cup sour cream
- 1½ teaspoons grated orange peel
- 1 tablespoon orange juice
- 1½ tablespoons minced crystallized ginger
- 3 ripe papayas

Place coconut in a wide frying pan and stir over low heat until golden brown (5 to 8 minutes). Let cool. Pour into a small serving bowl, cover, and set aside.

In another small serving bowl, stir together sour cream, orange peel, orange juice, and ginger. Cover and refrigerate for at least 1 hour.

Peel and seed papayas; cut fruit into bite-size chunks and place in a bowl. Present bowls of papaya, sour cream mixture, and coconut at the table. To eat, spear a papaya chunk with a fork; dip in sour cream mixture, then in coconut. Makes 6 servings.

Per serving: 3 grams protein, 28 grams carbohydrates, 12 grams total fat, 17 milligrams cholesterol, 59 milligrams sodium.

Hawaiian Fruit Delight

(Pictured on facing page)
Preparation time: 40 to 50 minutes

Calories per serving (including dressing): 183

Fresh pineapple shells make attractive "boats" for a tropical fruit medley topped with minted yogurt dressing.

- 1 small ripe pineapple (about 3½ lbs.)
- 1 large ripe papaya
- 1 orange
- ¼ cup chopped pitted dates
  Yogurt-Mint Dressing (recipe follows)
- 2 bananas
- ¼ cup chopped macadamia nuts or other nuts
- ¼ cup sweetened or unsweetened shredded coconut

Cut pineapple in half lengthwise through crown. With a small, sharp knife, cut fruit out of shells; set shells aside. Trim away core, then cut fruit into bite-size chunks and place in a large bowl.

Peel and halve papaya. Scoop out seeds, reserving 1 tablespoon seeds for dressing, if desired; cut fruit into bite-size chunks and add to pineapple in bowl. Using a sharp knife, cut peel and all white membrane from orange. Hold fruit over bowl to catch juice; cut segments free, lift out, and place in bowl. Add dates; mix gently. (At this point, you may cover and refrigerate fruit mixture and pineapple shells separately for up to 4 hours.)

Prepare Yogurt-Mint Dressing; cover and refrigerate.

To serve, slice bananas and mix gently into fruit in bowl; pile fruit mixture into pineapple shells. Sprinkle with macadamia nuts and coconut. Pass dressing to spoon over fruit. Makes 6 to 8 servings.

Yogurt-Mint Dressing. In a bowl, blend ¾ cup **plain lowfat yogurt,** 1 tablespoon **honey,** and 1 tablespoon chopped **fresh mint** or 1½ teaspoons crumbled dry mint. Crush reserved 1 tablespoon **papaya seeds** (if used); stir into dressing.

Per serving (including dressing): 3 grams protein, 36 grams carbohydrates, 5 grams total fat, 1 milligram cholesterol, 24 milligrams sodium.

Go native for dessert with this fresh and healthful tropical treat. It's Hawaiian Fruit Delight (recipe on facing page), a juicy mélange of island specialties. Serve it with a minted honey-yogurt dressing alongside.

· ·

Soufflés, Custards, Puddings & Soups

SMOOTH & ELEGANT CREATIONS

· ·

If you enjoy sweets that are soothingly smooth, the following desserts are just right for you. Some are lavish, such as Zabaglione over Clouds and Cold Coffee Soufflé; some are homey and old-fashioned, like Nutmeg Custard and Yogurt Rice Pudding. In addition, we offer recipes for molded puddings, a sparkling gelatin, and unusual dessert soups.

Because many of these recipes call for eggs, buttermilk, yogurt, milk, and fresh fruit, they are high in essential nutrients as well as light and delicious. Whether you're presenting a sweet ending for a family supper or adding the crowning touch to a company feast, you'll find plenty of food for thought in the following pages.

Lemon Angel Delight

Preparation time: 25 to 30 minutes
Baking time: 45 to 60 minutes

Calories per serving: 192

This baked pudding is like old-fashioned lemon sponge pie without the crust. In the oven, it separates into layers—a creamy custard on the bottom, an airy sponge on top.

- 2 lemons
- 3 eggs, separated
- 1 cup sugar
- ¼ cup all-purpose flour
- ⅛ teaspoon salt
- 2 tablespoons butter or margarine, melted
- 1½ cups lowfat milk

Grate enough peel from 1 of the lemons to make 1 teaspoon. Then squeeze juice from both lemons; you should have about ½ cup. Set peel and juice aside.

In a bowl, beat egg whites until they hold stiff peaks. Set aside. In another bowl, mix sugar, flour, and salt; stir in butter, lemon peel, and lemon juice. In a cup, lightly beat egg yolks; stir into sugar mixture along with milk, then beat with a rotary beater until smooth and creamy. Fold in egg whites. Divide mixture evenly among 8 buttered 4-ounce custard cups or pour all of mixture into a buttered 1-quart casserole.

Set a baking pan (large enough to hold custard cups or casserole) on center rack of a 350° oven. Arrange custard cups or casserole in pan, then pour boiling water into pan to come up halfway around cups or casserole. Bake, uncovered, until top is deep brown (about 45 minutes for custard cups, 1 hour for casserole). Serve warm or cooled. Makes 8 servings.

Per serving: 4 grams protein, 32 grams carbohydrates, 6 grams total fat, 114 milligrams cholesterol, 113 milligrams sodium.

Nutmeg Custard

Preparation time: 10 to 15 minutes
Baking time: about 45 minutes

Calories per serving: 170

Smooth, silky custard with a fragrant dusting of nutmeg is an old-fashioned dessert that has never lost its popularity. Serve it hot or cold—topped with fresh berries or other fruit, if you wish. Try serving leftover custard for breakfast with bran muffins or toast; it's a tasty and nutritious way to start the day.

- 4 cups lowfat milk
- 6 eggs
- ½ cup sugar
- 1 teaspoon vanilla
  Freshly grated nutmeg

In a 1½-quart pan, heat milk until steaming. Meanwhile, in a large bowl, beat eggs, sugar, and vanilla until well blended but not frothy. Gradually stir in steaming milk. Pour mixture into a shallow 1½-quart baking dish; sprinkle with nutmeg.

Set a 9- by 13-inch baking pan on center rack of a 350° oven. Set dish of custard mixture in pan, then pour boiling water into pan to come halfway up sides of dish. Bake, uncovered, until center of custard jiggles only slightly when dish is gently shaken (about 45 minutes).

Remove custard from hot water. Let stand for 10 minutes, then serve; or cover and refrigerate until cold. Makes 8 servings.

Per serving: 9 grams protein, 19 grams carbohydrates, 7 grams total fat, 215 milligrams cholesterol, 113 milligrams sodium.

Champagne Zabaglione

Preparation time: 5 to 10 minutes
Cooking time: about 5 minutes

Calories per serving: 189

This foamy, sparkling version of zabaglione is made with champagne and served over fresh orange sections.

- 2 large oranges
- 4 egg yolks
- ⅓ cup sugar
- 1 cup champagne or other sparkling white wine

Using a sharp knife, cut peel and all white membrane from oranges. Cut segments free and lift them out (or cut fruit into slices). Place ¼ of the oranges in each of 4 stemmed glasses. Set aside.

In a round-bottomed zabaglione pan or in the top of a double boiler, beat together egg yolks, sugar, and ¾ cup of the champagne. Place round-bottomed pan over medium-high heat or set double boiler over boiling water. Beat mixture constantly with a wire whisk or a portable electric mixer until very foamy and thick enough to hold soft peaks (about 5 minutes). Remove from heat.

At once, pour remaining ¼ cup champagne equally over oranges and top equally with zabaglione. Makes 4 servings.

Per serving: 3 grams protein, 30 grams carbohydrates, 6 grams total fat, 272 milligrams cholesterol, 11 milligrams sodium.

Beneath a coat of golden caramel, Flan (recipe on facing page) is a silky-smooth custard
made from milk, sugar, and eggs. Traditionally served after
a Mexican meal, it's just as good a finale for other kinds of food.

. . . .

Zabaglione over Clouds

Preparation time: 25 to 30 minutes
Cooking time: about 15 minutes

Calories per serving: 181

Traditional Italian *Zabaglione* is a hot, frothy pudding made with Marsala wine. In this dramatic dessert, warm zabaglione is poured over soft clouds of poached meringue that float in berry purée. The meringues and purée can be made ahead; prepare the zabaglione at the last minute, then serve with a flourish.

- 4 **egg whites**
- ½ **teaspoon cream of tartar**
  About ½ cup sugar
- 3 **cups hulled strawberries**
  Classic Zabaglione (recipe follows)

In large bowl of an electric mixer, beat egg whites and cream of tartar until foamy. Gradually add ⅓ cup of the sugar and continue to beat until mixture holds stiff, moist peaks. Fill a deep 10- to 12-inch frying pan with about 1 inch of water. Bring to a simmer over medium heat. Reduce heat so bubbles do not break the surface.

With a large spoon and a spatula, shape meringue into 6 oval mounds; slide 3 of the mounds into water. Cook, uncovered, until meringues feel set when lightly touched (about 4 minutes), turning over once. Lift out meringues with a slotted spoon and drain on a rack; gently pat dry with paper towels. Repeat to cook remaining 3 meringues. If made ahead, cover on racks and refrigerate for up to 24 hours.

Set aside 6 of the prettiest strawberries. In a blender or food processor, whirl remaining strawberries until puréed. Pour through a fine wire strainer set over a bowl; discard seeds. Sweeten purée with about 3 tablespoons sugar (or to taste). If made ahead, cover and refrigerate until next day.

Place equal portions of berry purée on 6 dessert plates; tilt plates to spread sauce. Set a meringue on each plate. Garnish with reserved strawberries, whole or sliced.

Prepare zabaglione; at the table or in the kitchen, pour hot zabaglione over each meringue. Serve at once. Makes 6 servings.

Classic Zabaglione. In a round-bottomed zabaglione pan or in the top of a double boiler, beat together 6 **egg yolks,** 2 tablespoons **sugar,** and ⅓ cup **dry or sweet Marsala** or sherry. Place round-bottomed pan over very low heat (if using an electric element, heat element to low before setting pan in place). If using a double boiler, set over gently simmering water. Beat mixture constantly with a wire whisk or a portable electric mixer just until thick enough to retain a slight peak briefly when whisk or beaters are withdrawn (3 to 6 minutes). Taste for sweetness; if desired, beat in 1 more tablespoon **sugar.** Use hot.

Per serving: 5 grams protein, 27 grams carbohydrates, 6 grams total fat, 272 milligrams cholesterol, 43 milligrams sodium.

Flan

(Pictured on facing page)
Preparation time: 15 to 20 minutes
Baking time: about 40 minutes
Chilling time: 3 to 4 hours

Calories per serving: 213

A sheath of golden caramel gives this classic Mexican dessert its characteristic flavor and also eases unmolding. Serve it with hot, strong coffee for a tempting finale to a Spanish- or Mexican-style meal.

- ⅓ **cup sugar**
- 6 **eggs**
- 6 **tablespoons sugar**
- 1 **teaspoon vanilla**
- 2 **cups lowfat milk**

Spread the ⅓ cup sugar in a small frying pan with a nonstick finish. Cook over medium heat just until sugar is completely melted and a clear amber in color; shake and tilt pan often to mix sugar as it begins to liquefy and caramelize.

Immediately pour syrup, all at once, into a straight-sided 1-quart baking dish. Tilt dish so syrup coats bottom and ½ inch up sides. Set dish on a rack; caramel will harden rapidly.

In a large bowl, beat eggs, the 6 tablespoons sugar, and vanilla until well blended but not frothy. Add milk; stir well. Pour egg mixture into caramel-coated dish.

Set a 9- or 10-inch square baking pan on center rack of a 350° oven. Set dish of flan mixture in pan, then pour boiling water into pan to a depth of about 1 inch. Bake, uncovered, until center of flan jiggles only slightly when dish is gently shaken (about 40 minutes).

Remove flan from hot water; let cool on a rack for 15 minutes, then cover and refrigerate until cold or for up to 2 days (caramel liquefies as flan cools).

To serve, run a knife tip around edge of flan. Invert a rimmed serving plate over flan; hold plate and dish together and invert both. Lift off dish; caramel will flow over flan. Cut into wedges and spoon caramel over each serving. Makes 6 servings.

Per serving: 9 grams protein, 28 grams carbohydrates, 7 grams total fat, 280 milligrams cholesterol, 110 milligrams sodium.

Tapioca Orange Parfaits

Preparation time: about 45 minutes
Chilling time: 2 to 3 hours

Calories per serving: 238

For a make-ahead dessert with a pretty effect, layer fresh oranges and tapioca pudding in parfait glasses.

    3   tablespoons quick-cooking tapioca
    ⅓   cup sugar
    ⅛   teaspoon salt
    1   egg, beaten
    2¾ cups lowfat milk
    ¾   teaspoon vanilla
    2   large oranges

In a pan, stir together tapioca, sugar, salt, egg, and milk; let stand for 5 minutes. Then bring to a full boil over medium heat, stirring constantly. Remove from heat and stir in vanilla. Let cool, uncovered; stir once after 20 minutes.

Using a sharp knife, cut peel and all white membrane from oranges; cut segments free and lift out. Layer cooled tapioca and orange segments in four 8-ounce parfait glasses. Cover and refrigerate until cold before serving. Makes 4 servings.

Per serving: 8 grams protein, 42 grams carbohydrates, 5 grams total fat, 82 milligrams cholesterol, 171 milligrams sodium.

Strawberry Bavarian

Preparation time: about 1½ hours
Chilling time: at least 4 hours

Calories per serving: 154

Fluffy Bavarian creams are a natural choice when you want a rich-tasting dessert that's not too heavy.

    2   cups sliced hulled strawberries
    ½   cup sugar
    1   envelope unflavored gelatin
    ¾   cup cold water
    2   egg whites
    1   cup whipping cream

Place strawberries and sugar in a bowl. Partially crush berries with a fork or potato masher (there should still be some berry chunks); set aside.

In a 1-quart pan, sprinkle gelatin over cold water and let stand for about 5 minutes to soften. Stir in berry mixture. Bring just to a boil, stirring constantly; then pour into a large bowl and let cool until thick but not set.

In small bowl of an electric mixer, beat egg whites until they hold stiff peaks. Fold into berry mixture. Pour cream into mixer bowl; beat until cream holds soft peaks, then fold into berry mixture.

Divide mixture equally among 8 dessert glasses. Cover and refrigerate until set (at least 4 hours) or until next day. Makes 8 servings.

Per serving: 2 grams protein, 16 grams carbohydrates, 9 grams total fat, 33 milligrams cholesterol, 24 milligrams sodium.

Creamy Cantaloupe Mousse

Preparation time: about 2 hours
Chilling time: at least 4 hours

Calories per serving: 234

A favorite breakfast fruit makes a surprise appearance for dessert in this delicate molded mousse.

    2   small cantaloupes
    1   envelope unflavored gelatin
    ⅓   cup sugar
    ¼   teaspoon salt
    1   teaspoon grated lemon peel
    3   tablespoons lemon juice
    1   teaspoon vanilla
    1   cup whipping cream

Cut 1 of the cantaloupes in half; scoop out and discard seeds, cut off and discard rind, and cut fruit into chunks. In a blender or food processor, whirl enough melon chunks to make 1½ cups purée. Set aside. Discard seeds and rind from remaining cantaloupe; scoop out fruit with a melon baller or cut into cubes. Cover and refrigerate melon balls and any melon chunks not used for purée.

In a small pan, mix gelatin, sugar, and salt; stir in puréed melon. Let mixture stand for 1 minute, then stir over low heat until gelatin is completely dissolved (about 5 minutes). Stir in lemon peel, lemon juice, and vanilla. Transfer to large bowl of an electric mixer; refrigerate until partially set.

Beat gelatin mixture on high speed until thick and fluffy. Refrigerate until mixture mounds slightly when dropped from a spoon. In small bowl of mixer, beat cream until it holds soft peaks; fold into gelatin mixture along with 1 cup of the melon balls. Spoon into a 4-cup mold, cover, and refrigerate until set.

To serve, dip mold up to rim in hottest tap water; then invert a serving plate over mold. Hold plate and mold together; invert both and shake gently to loosen. Lift off mold. Garnish mousse with remaining melon balls (and chunks, if desired). Makes 6 servings.

Per serving: 3 grams protein, 24 grams carbohydrates, 15 grams total fat, 54 milligrams cholesterol, 120 milligrams sodium.

Holiday Cranberry Mousse

Preparation time: 20 to 30 minutes
Chilling time: at least 7 hours

Calories per serving: 211

Wedges of this rosy mousse make a marvelous holiday dessert. Sweet raspberries balance the tartness of the cranberries; orange-flavored liqueur adds extra zest. For a festive presentation, decorate the mousse with fresh cranberries and sprigs of holly.

- 2 **envelopes unflavored gelatin**
- ½ **cup sugar**
- 1 **package (10 oz.) frozen sweetened raspberries, thawed**
- 2 **cups (½ lb.) fresh or frozen cranberries**
- 2 **tablespoons orange-flavored liqueur or thawed frozen orange juice concentrate**
- ½ **cup whipping cream**

In a 2½- to 3-quart pan, stir together gelatin and sugar.

Pour thawed raspberries and their juice into a 4-cup measuring cup and add enough water to make 3 cups total. Stir raspberry mixture and cranberries into gelatin mixture. Bring to a boil over medium-high heat, stirring; then reduce heat and simmer, uncovered, for 5 minutes. Remove from heat and stir in liqueur.

Cover mixture and refrigerate until it has the consistency of unbeaten egg whites (about 3 hours). In a small bowl, beat cream until it holds soft peaks, then fold into gelatin mixture. Spoon into a 6-cup mold; cover and refrigerate until mousse is set (at least 4 hours) or for up to 2 days.

To unmold, dip mold up to rim in hottest tap water, then invert a serving plate over mold. Hold plate and mold together; invert both and shake gently to loosen. Lift off mold. Makes 6 servings.

Per serving: 3 grams protein, 36 grams carbohydrates, 6 grams total fat, 22 milligrams cholesterol, 10 milligrams sodium.

Demi-chocolate Mousses

Preparation time: 5 to 10 minutes
Chilling time: at least 3 hours

Calories per serving: 209

For indulgence on a small scale, try these little mousses, served in demitasse cups like French *pots de crème*. They make a dainty dessert for chocolate lovers who don't want to throw caution entirely to the winds. In addition, they're marvelously easy to prepare.

- 1 **egg**
- 1 **package (6 oz.) semisweet chocolate chips**
- 2 **tablespoons sugar**
- 1 **teaspoon vanilla**
  Dash of salt
- ¾ **cup lowfat milk**
  About ½ cup Whipped Topping (page 41) or whipped cream

Place egg, chocolate chips, sugar, vanilla, and salt in a blender. In a small pan, heat milk just until simmering; pour into blender. Whirl on low speed for 1 minute, then pour mixture equally into six 4-ounce demitasse cups. Cover; refrigerate until firm (at least 3 hours). To serve, top mousses equally with Whipped Topping. Makes 6 servings.

Per serving: 4 grams protein, 24 grams carbohydrates, 13 grams total fat, 48 milligrams cholesterol, 56 milligrams sodium.

Salzburger Nockerln

Preparation time: 30 to 40 minutes
Baking time: 10 to 12 minutes

Calories per serving: 132

Something like a soufflé, this traditional Austrian dessert features a billowy froth of whipped sweetened eggs, briefly baked, and topped with melting chocolate curls.

- 1 **ounce semisweet chocolate**
- 4 **eggs, separated**
- ¼ **cup sugar**
- 4 **teaspoons all-purpose flour**
- 1 **tablespoon butter or margarine**

Using a vegetable peeler, shave chocolate or make chocolate curls; set aside.

In large bowl of an electric mixer, beat egg whites until they hold soft peaks. Gradually add sugar, beating until mixture holds very stiff peaks. Set aside.

In small bowl of mixer, beat egg yolks on high speed until very light in color and slightly thickened. Gradually add flour, beating until mixture is thick and well blended. Fold yolks into whites, blending lightly but thoroughly.

In a shallow oval or rectangular pan (about 7 by 11 inches), melt butter over direct medium heat. Heap egg mixture into pan, making 6 equal mounds. Bake, uncovered, in a 350° oven until top is pale brown (10 to 12 minutes). Sprinkle with chocolate and serve immediately. Makes 6 servings.

Per serving: 4 grams protein, 13 grams carbohydrates, 7 grams total fat, 188 milligrams cholesterol, 66 milligrams sodium.

Strawberries-and-Cream Soufflé

(Pictured on facing page)
Preparation time: 1½ to 2 hours
Chilling time: about 6 hours

Calories per serving: 229

Ribbons of fresh strawberry sauce weave through this creamy cold soufflé. Prepare it in a glass bowl or soufflé dish, so that its pretty layered appearance can be admired by all.

 1 **envelope plus 1 teaspoon unflavored gelatin**
 ¾ **cup sugar**
 ½ **cup lowfat milk**
 3 **eggs, separated**
  Strawberry purée (directions follow)
 1 **cup whipping cream**
  Quartered hulled strawberries (optional)
  Thin orange slices and mint sprigs (optional)

In a small pan, stir together 1 envelope gelatin and ¼ cup of the sugar. Stir in milk and egg yolks; cook over low heat, stirring constantly, until gelatin is completely dissolved (about 7 minutes). Cover and refrigerate until mixture mounds slightly when dropped from a spoon.

Meanwhile, prepare strawberry purée.

To make strawberry sauce, stir together remaining 1 teaspoon gelatin and ¼ cup of the sugar in a small pan; stir in 1¼ cups of the strawberry purée. Bring to a boil, stirring; let cool. Set aside.

To make soufflé mixture, in large bowl of an electric mixer, beat egg whites until they hold soft peaks. Gradually add remaining ¼ cup sugar and continue to beat until mixture holds stiff peaks. Turn cooled egg yolk mixture into another bowl and beat until smooth; add cream and beat until mixture holds soft peaks. Fold cream mixture into egg white mixture along with remaining ¾ cup strawberry purée.

To assemble, fold a 26-inch length of foil into quarters lengthwise. Wrap this collar around a 4- to 6-cup soufflé dish or glass bowl, letting it extend 2 inches above dish rim; secure with string. Spoon ⅓ of the soufflé mixture into dish and spread evenly, then top evenly with half the strawberry sauce. Layer on half the remaining soufflé mixture, remaining strawberry sauce, and remaining soufflé mixture. Smooth top; cover and refrigerate until firm (about 6 hours). Remove collar before serving; garnish soufflé with quartered strawberries, orange slices, and mint, if desired. Makes 8 servings.

Strawberry purée. In a blender or food processor, whirl 5 cups sliced hulled **strawberries** until coarsely mashed. Stir in 2 tablespoons **lemon juice** and ½ teaspoon grated **lemon peel.** You should have 2 cups purée.

Per serving: 5 grams protein, 27 grams carbohydrates, 12 grams total fat, 137 milligrams cholesterol, 46 milligrams sodium.

Cold Lemon Soufflé

Preparation time: 45 to 60 minutes
Chilling time: at least 4 hours

Calories per serving: 229

A "rose" made from a spiral of lemon peel would make an elegant garnish for this chilled soufflé. For an appealing contrast of colors and flavors, offer sliced purple plums or small bunches of red grapes with each serving.

 1 **envelope unflavored gelatin**
 1 **cup sugar**
 ¼ **cup cold water**
 4 **eggs, separated**
 2 **teaspoons grated lemon peel**
 ½ **cup lemon juice**
 1 **cup whipping cream**
  Sliced purple plums or small bunches of red grapes

Combine gelatin, ½ cup of the sugar, and cold water in the top of a double boiler; beat in egg yolks, lemon peel, and lemon juice until well blended. Set over boiling water and cook, stirring, just until mixture coats a metal spoon in a thin, even, velvety layer. Remove from heat; let cool to room temperature.

In large bowl of an electric mixer, beat egg whites until they hold soft peaks. Gradually add remaining ½ cup sugar; continue to beat until mixture holds stiff, moist peaks. Set aside. In small bowl of mixer, beat cream until it holds soft peaks.

Fold whipped cream and cooled lemon mixture into beaten egg whites just until blended; spoon into a 4- to 6-cup soufflé dish. (If necessary, make a collar for soufflé dish: fold a 26-inch length of foil into quarters lengthwise and wrap it around dish, letting foil extend 2 inches above dish rim. Secure with string.)

Cover soufflé and refrigerate until firm (at least 4 hours). Remove collar (if used) before serving; offer fruit to accompany soufflé. Makes 8 servings.

Per serving: 4 grams protein, 27 grams carbohydrates, 12 grams total fat, 170 milligrams cholesterol, 49 milligrams sodium.

Strawberries and cream are an age-old combination, but never so tempting as in
Strawberries-and-Cream Soufflé (recipe on facing page). This elegant cold dessert owes its
striking good looks to alternating layers of creamy soufflé and fresh strawberry sauce.

. . . .

Thick and velvety smooth, home-made yogurt is a delicious alternative to store-bought—and it costs much less. Enjoy it plain or lightly sweetened, on its own or as a low-calorie topping for your favorite desserts.

Our yogurt is generously fortified with nonfat dry milk, so it has more protein yet only about half the fat of most commercial lowfat yogurts. And because it's thick and additive-free, it's easily turned into a tangy cheese simply by draining off the whey. This yogurt cheese is smooth and creamy, like cream cheese; try it with fresh fruit or as a spread for sweet crackers or tea bread.

To make your own yogurt, you need only milk, a small amount of commercial yogurt to use as starter, and a means of maintaining the mixture at about 115°F while it thickens.

Getting Started

When you make yogurt—as when you bake bread—you must work with living organisms. Temperatures above 120°F will kill them; below 105°F, their action is slowed considerably. They work fastest at around 115°F, and other things being equal, the more quickly the action proceeds, the less tart the finished yogurt will be.

You'll need an accurate thermometer that measures in the 100° to 120°F range, as do standard dairy thermometers and some meat, candy, and deep-frying thermometers. Before using any thermometer, test it for accuracy: it should register 212°F when inserted into boiling water at sea level, 203°F at 5,000 feet.

Before you begin your first batch of yogurt, test the method you plan to use for keeping it warm (see "Warming Methods").

Simply fill the yogurt containers with water at 115°F and follow directions as if making yogurt. If using a vacuum bottle, leave it undisturbed for about 3 hours, then check the water temperature; it shouldn't fall much below 105°F. If you find it has cooled too quickly, try again with the bottle wrapped in a warm blanket or towel. If using an electric appliance, check the water temperature often for up to 2 hours; if necessary, adjust the heat setting to hold the temperature between 110° and 115°F, then mark the spot on the dial.

No two yogurts taste exactly alike, so for your starter, select a yogurt you know and like. It must be fresh, since the organisms become less active as yogurt ages. After your first batch, you can use your own yogurt for a starter, but it, too, must be fresh—not more than 1 week old.

Our recipe calls for either instant or noninstant nonfat dry milk powder; the noninstant type is more concentrated, so a smaller amount is required. We've found that additive-free, noninstant milk gives the best-tasting result. Look for it in health food stores. Whichever dry milk you use, sniff it for freshness—it should be almost odor-free.

When you start the yogurt, make sure that all the equipment that comes in contact with the milk is dishwasher-clean or scalded to prevent any bacterial action that could interfere with the action of the yogurt starter.

Try not to disturb the yogurt while it's being made; too much motion can slow or even stop the action. Once the yogurt is softly set, though, it can be removed from the heat source and refrigerated (it will thicken as it chills).

Warming Methods

You don't need fancy equipment to make yogurt. For years, people have had great success simply setting the cultured milk in a warm spot near the hot water heater or pilot light or wrapping the container in something like a thermal blanket.

There are, however, a number of commercial yogurt makers available. Some are electrically heated; others are essentially well-insulated containers. Some models make up to 2 quarts at a time. Though these units take much of the thermometer-watching out of the process, they often include a dairy thermometer for use when heating the milk to 115°F before adding the starter.

Among the make-do methods we tested for keeping things warm, we had the most reliable results with electric appliances and good-quality wide-mouth vacuum bottles. If you're new to yogurt making or have had failures in the past, we suggest you try either of these methods or consider buying a yogurt maker.

Electric appliances. To use an electric frying pan or griddle, use a bowl or several canning jars for the yogurt containers. Set containers inside a large, deep pan; then set this pan in the frying pan or on the griddle.

To preheat the system, fill yogurt containers with water at 115°F; set them in the deep pan and add water at 115°F to come up around containers. Place a thermometer in the water surrounding the yogurt containers and turn the appliance setting to "warm" (or whatever setting will keep the water at 115°F).

Cover pan with lid or, if containers are large, cover with a tent of foil. (You can also set a folded bath towel on top of the foil to help hold in heat.) Let stand while you heat the milk. After adding the starter to the milk mixture, remove yogurt containers, pour out the water, and replace with yogurt mixture; return containers to pan. For finished yogurt with the most even consistency, have the surrounding water at the same level as the yogurt inside the containers (several small jars are easier to handle than a single large jar or bowl).

Leave the system undisturbed until the yogurt has set (3½ to 5 hours). If the water temperature should go as high as 120°F, quickly ladle out some of it, replace with cold water, and reduce heat setting as needed. Refrigerate the finished yogurt.

Vacuum bottles. Preheat a 1- or 2-quart wide-mouth vacuum bottle by filling it with water at 115°F. Cap it and let stand while you heat the milk. Pour water out of the container and immediately replace it with the milk mixture at 115°F. Replace cap tightly and leave undisturbed for about 4 hours. Check; if yogurt has not set, recap quickly and test again every 30 minutes. When yogurt is set, remove cap from bottle, cover loosely, and refrigerate.

Yogurt-making appliances. Follow the manufacturer's directions for operating the unit. Though the directions may not suggest it, we recommend preheating (it shortens the culturing time, often by several hours, and results in yogurt that's less tart).

Fill the container with water at 115°F; then turn on electric units or cover nonelectric ones while heating the milk. Then pour out the water and immediately replace with the milk mixture at 115°F.

Reset unit and leave undisturbed until yogurt is set (3½ to 5 hours). Turn off or remove from heat and refrigerate.

Thick Homemade Yogurt

. . . .

¼ **cup fresh, plain yogurt**

2 **cups fluid lowfat or nonfat milk**

¾ **cup noninstant nonfat dry milk or 1⅓ cups instant nonfat dry milk powder**

Measure yogurt into a small dish and set it in a pan of warm (about 115°F) water; stir occasionally. Preheat yogurt maker or container as directed for the warming method you plan to use.

Set fluid milk in a pan over medium heat; or pour into a glass bowl and heat in a microwave oven at **HIGH (100%)**, using the probe if your oven has one. Heat to scalding (about 185°F). Remove from heat and let cool; discard scum from top of milk.

Meanwhile, pour about ½ cup hot water into a blender. Add dry milk. Whirl on lowest speed, using on-off pulses and scraping sides often, just until smooth but not foamy. Measure, then add cold water to make 1¾ cups. Add this mixture to the fluid milk, then check its temperature.

As soon as milk mixture has cooled to 115°F, add a few spoonfuls to warm yogurt and stir until smooth. Pour yogurt into milk mixture and mix until smooth. Skim off any foam with a slotted spoon and transfer mixture to preheated yogurt container. Keep warm as directed for the method you are using. When set (usually in 3½ to 5 hours), remove from heat; refrigerate, covered, until cold. Makes 1 quart.

Lightly Sweetened Yogurt

Follow directions for **Thick Homemade Yogurt,** but scald milk with about 3 tablespoons **honey** or ¼ to ⅓ cup (to taste) granulated or firmly packed brown sugar. After milk has cooled, add 2 teaspoons **vanilla,** if desired.

Yogurt Cheese

Wring out a clean dishcloth or three or four 20-inch squares of cheesecloth in cold water. Line a colander with the cloth. Spoon in 1 quart **Thick Homemade Yogurt.** Twist ends of cloth together to close. Place colander in the sink (or set in a large pan or bowl) and let drain at room temperature until yogurt has the consistency of cream cheese (about 24 hours). Cover and refrigerate. Makes 1½ cups.

Sweet Yogurt Cheese

Prepare **Yogurt Cheese;** blend in 1 tablespoon **sweet sherry,** brandy, or orange-flavored liqueur *or* 2 tablespoons thawed frozen orange juice concentrate. Mix in **sugar** or honey to taste; stir in 3 tablespoons finely chopped **nuts** (optional). Serve with fresh fruit, scones, or tea bread.

Orange Sauce

Prepare **Sweet Yogurt Cheese** with orange-flavored liqueur or orange juice concentrate. Thin to desired consistency with **milk** or water. Serve with fruit desserts, plain cake, or fruit salad.

Pineapple Sauce

Prepare **Yogurt Cheese;** blend in 1 can (about 8 oz.) **crushed pineapple** (drained) and sweeten to taste with **sugar** or honey. Thin with **milk** or pineapple juice. Serve with plain cake or fruit salad.

For a company dessert, it's hard to beat Cold Coffee Soufflé (recipe on facing page) with a fancy chocolate garnish. Its dressy appearance, melt-in-the-mouth texture, and beguiling mocha flavor make it a winner on all counts.

· ·

Cold Coffee Soufflé

(Pictured on facing page)

Preparation time: about 1¼ hours
Chilling time: at least 1 hour

Calories per serving: 130

For all its lavish looks, this creamy, rich-tasting party dessert can be enjoyed with only modest calorie intake.

- 1½ to 2 tablespoons **instant coffee**
- ½ cup **hot water**
  Ice water
- 1 envelope **unflavored gelatin**
- 4 teaspoons **cold water**
- ⅓ cup **boiling water**
- 1⅓ cups **instant nonfat dry milk powder**
- 6 tablespoons **sugar**
- ⅓ cup **salad oil**
- 1 teaspoon **vanilla**
- 2 teaspoons **lemon juice**
- 3 tablespoons **coffee-flavored liqueur** or **rum** (optional)
  Chocolate decoration (directions follow), optional

In a 2-cup glass measure, combine coffee and hot water; stir until coffee is dissolved. Then add enough ice water to make 1 cup liquid. Refrigerate until very cold; also refrigerate beaters and large bowl of an electric mixer until cold.

In a cup, sprinkle gelatin over the 4 teaspoons cold water and let stand for about 5 minutes to soften. Add boiling water and stir until gelatin is completely dissolved. Let cool to room temperature (if mixture sets before you're ready to use it, set cup in a pan of hot water to soften gelatin again).

Combine chilled coffee mixture and dry milk in chilled mixer bowl. Beat on high speed until mixture holds soft peaks (about 5 minutes); if mixture spatters, drape a towel or wax paper loosely over bowl and beaters. Gradually add sugar, beating constantly. Scrape down bowl sides; continue to beat, gradually pouring in oil, vanilla, lemon juice, gelatin mixture, and liqueur (if used). Scrape down bowl sides; beat for 1 more minute.

Fold a 26-inch length of foil into quarters lengthwise and wrap around a 4-cup soufflé dish, letting foil extend about 1 inch above dish rim. Secure with string. Pour coffee mixture into dish, cover, and refrigerate for at least 1 hour or until next day.

Garnish with chocolate decoration, if desired. Remove collar before serving. Makes 10 servings.

Chocolate decoration. Melt about 2 ounces **semisweet chocolate** in the top of a double boiler over simmering water, stirring constantly. Fill a large spoon with melted chocolate; tilt spoon above soufflé and move it quickly back and forth, shaking spoon to create a "spatter" pattern.

For the chocolate curls, draw a vegetable peeler firmly across a thick block of **semisweet chocolate.** (If chocolate is too cold to make long curls, warm it briefly over a light bulb or an electric element set on low.) Carefully arrange chocolate curls in center of soufflé, standing curls upright.

If desired, refrigerate soufflé briefly to firm chocolate spatters before serving.

Per serving: 4 grams protein, 13 grams carbohydrates, 7 grams total fat, 2 milligrams cholesterol, 51 milligrams sodium.

Cold Apricot Soufflé

In a pan, combine 1 cup **moist-pack dried apricots** and 2¼ cups **water.** Bring to a boil over high heat; then reduce heat, cover, and simmer until apricots are tender to bite (about 20 minutes). Pour fruit and liquid into a blender or food processor; add 2 tablespoons **sugar**, 1 tablespoon **lemon juice**, 1 teaspoon **ground cinnamon**, and ¼ teaspoon **ground cloves.** Whirl until puréed. Cover and refrigerate until cold.

Follow directions for **Cold Coffee Soufflé,** but omit instant coffee and hot water; instead, just beat dry milk together with 1 cup **ice water** in place of chilled coffee mixture. Omit liqueur. After beating in gelatin, place mixture (still in mixer bowl) in freezer for 10 to 15 minutes. Then remove from freezer, add apricot mixture, and beat on low speed until well blended.

Prepare soufflé dish, pour in apricot mixture, and refrigerate as directed for **Cold Coffee Soufflé.** Omit chocolate decoration; instead, garnish soufflé with 2 tablespoons finely chopped **nuts.**

Cold Pumpkin Soufflé

Follow directions for **Cold Coffee Soufflé,** but omit instant coffee and hot water; instead, just beat dry milk together with 1 cup **ice water** in place of chilled coffee mixture. Omit liqueur. After beating in gelatin, place mixture (still in mixer bowl) in freezer for 10 to 15 minutes.

In a bowl, combine 1¼ cups **canned solid-pack pumpkin;** ⅓ cup firmly packed **brown sugar;** 1 teaspoon **ground cinnamon;** ½ teaspoon *each* **salt, ground nutmeg,** and **ground ginger;** and ¼ teaspoon **ground cloves.** Remove gelatin mixture from freezer, add pumpkin mixture, and beat on low speed until blended.

Prepare soufflé dish, pour in pumpkin mixture, and refrigerate as directed for **Cold Coffee Soufflé.** Omit chocolate decoration; instead, garnish soufflé with 2 tablespoons finely chopped **nuts.**

Shimmering Strawberry Goblets

Preparation time: 10 to 15 minutes
Chilling time: at least 2 hours

Calories per serving: 113

Here's an easy way to showcase fresh strawberries: suspend them in pretty glass goblets filled with clear grape juice gelatin.

- 1 **envelope unflavored gelatin**
- 2 **cups white grape juice**
  About 1½ cups halved hulled strawberries
- ½ **cup Whipped Topping (page 41) or whipped cream**

In a 1½- to 2-quart pan, sprinkle gelatin over grape juice and let stand for about 5 minutes to soften. Then stir over medium heat until gelatin is completely dissolved. Refrigerate just until mixture has the consistency of unbeaten egg whites (about 1 hour). Fold in strawberries, then spoon mixture equally into four 8-ounce stemmed glasses. Cover and refrigerate until set (at least 1 hour) or until next day. To serve, top each goblet with 2 tablespoons of the Whipped Topping. Makes 4 servings.

Per serving: 3 grams protein, 22 grams carbohydrates, 2 grams total fat, .32 milligram cholesterol, 15 milligrams sodium.

Fresh Cherry Soup

Preparation time: about 45 minutes
Cooking time: about 20 minutes
Chilling time: at least 6 hours

Calories per serving: 229

Made with white wine, cinnamon, and yogurt, this sweet Bing cherry soup is an especially sophisticated light dessert.

- 1½ **pounds Bing cherries, stemmed and pitted**
- 1 **cup *each* water and dry white wine**
- 1 **cinnamon stick (2 to 3 inches long)**
- 1½ **tablespoons lemon juice**
- ¼ **to ⅓ cup granulated sugar**
- 1 **tablespoon *each* cornstarch and water, stirred together**
- ¼ **cup kirsch (optional)**
- 1 **cup plain lowfat yogurt**
  Powdered sugar

In a 4-quart pan, combine cherries, water, wine, cinnamon stick, and lemon juice. Bring to a boil over high heat; then reduce heat, cover, and simmer until

fruit mashes easily (about 15 minutes). Remove from heat and discard cinnamon stick. With a slotted spoon, transfer fruit (leaving liquid in pan) to a food processor; whirl until puréed.

Return purée to pan; stir in granulated sugar and cornstarch mixture. Cook over high heat, stirring, until mixture is thickened (about 5 minutes). Remove from heat and let cool slightly. Skim off and discard any foam. Add kirsch (if used). Stir yogurt until smooth, then whisk half the yogurt into soup until smoothly incorporated. Let soup cool; cover and refrigerate for at least 6 hours.

Just before serving, sweeten remaining yogurt to taste with powdered sugar; spoon into a bowl. Pour soup equally into 4 bowls; pass sweetened yogurt and additional powdered sugar to add to each serving. Makes 4 servings.

Per serving: 5 grams protein, 51 grams carbohydrates, 2 grams total fat, 3 milligrams cholesterol, 44 milligrams sodium.

Chilled Citrus Consommé

Preparation time: 25 to 30 minutes
Chilling time: 1 to 2 hours

Calories per serving: 115

Simple jellied consommé, sweet and tangy with orange and grapefruit juices, makes an especially refreshing dessert.

- 2 **small grapefruits or large oranges**
- 1 **envelope unflavored gelatin**
- 2 **cups orange juice**
- 3 **tablespoons sugar**
- 3 **tablespoons lemon or lime juice**
  Mint sprigs

Cut peel and all white membrane from grapefruits. Hold fruit over a bowl to catch juice; cut segments free, lift out, and place in bowl. Set aside.

In a 2- to 3-quart pan, sprinkle gelatin over ½ cup of the orange juice; let stand for about 5 minutes to soften, then stir over low heat until gelatin is completely dissolved. Add remaining 1½ cups orange juice, sugar, and lemon juice and stir until sugar is dissolved. Remove from heat.

Reserve 4 of the grapefruit segments; cut remaining segments into bite-size pieces and add with any juices to gelatin mixture. Stir until blended. Cover and refrigerate until well chilled. Serve cold, stirring to break up if set (consommé should have the consistency of thick soup). Garnish with reserved grapefruit segments and mint. Makes 4 servings.

Per serving: 3 grams protein, 27 grams carbohydrates, .14 gram total fat, 0 milligram cholesterol, 5 milligrams sodium.

Sweet Buttermilk Soup

Preparation time: 30 to 40 minutes

Calories per serving: 197

In Scandinavia, Eastern Europe, and parts of Asia, fruit soups and other sweet soups are traditional favorites. This sweet-tart dessert soup is inspired by a Danish recipe; it's topped with fluffy meringue and fresh berries.

- 3 cups strawberries (hulled and sliced), raspberries, blueberries, or blackberries
  Honey or sugar (optional)
- 3 eggs, separated
  About ½ cup sugar
- 2 teaspoons vanilla
- 4 cups buttermilk
  Mint sprigs (optional)

Set aside ½ cup of the berries for garnish. Place remaining 2½ cups berries in a serving bowl; sweeten to taste with honey, if desired. Set aside.

In small bowl of an electric mixer, beat egg whites until foamy. Gradually add 3 tablespoons of the sugar and continue to beat until mixture holds stiff peaks. Set aside.

In large bowl of mixer, beat egg yolks until thick and lemon-colored. Gradually add up to about 6 tablespoons of the sugar (or to taste); beat until thick and smooth. Stir in vanilla and buttermilk. Sweeten to taste with more sugar, if desired.

Pour buttermilk mixture into a serving bowl. Top with spoonfuls of meringue and reserved ½ cup berries; garnish with mint, if desired. To serve, ladle soup and some of the meringue into each bowl; pass remaining berries at the table to spoon over individual servings. Makes 6 servings.

Per serving: 9 grams protein, 31 grams carbohydrates, 4 grams total fat, 144 milligrams cholesterol, 207 milligrams sodium.

Almond Buttermilk Soup

Follow directions for **Sweet Buttermilk Soup,** but omit vanilla; instead, add ¼ teaspoon **almond extract.** Sprinkle ¼ cup sliced **almonds** over soup with the ½ cup strawberries. Serve as directed.

Orange Buttermilk Soup

Follow directions for **Sweet Buttermilk Soup,** but omit vanilla; instead, add ¼ cup **orange-flavored liqueur** or thawed frozen orange juice concentrate. Sprinkle 1 teaspoon grated **orange peel** over soup with the ½ cup strawberries. Serve as directed.

Yogurt Rice Pudding

Preparation time: 30 to 60 minutes
Baking time: 30 to 60 minutes

Calories per serving: 210

Yogurt gives this baked rice pudding its pleasing tang. You can vary the recipe by using plain or flavored yogurt, white or brown rice.

If you like, spoon sweet and crunchy condiments over the warm pudding; choices include granola-type cereal, raisins, coconut, and chopped nuts. Like Nutmeg Custard (page 53), this nutritious pudding makes a satisfying breakfast dish as well as a tempting light dessert.

- 1⅓ to 1⅔ cups water
- ⅔ cup white or brown long-grain rice
- 2 eggs
- ½ cup sugar
- ½ teaspoon vanilla
- ¾ cup lowfat milk
- 1 cup plain or vanilla-, orange-, or lemon-flavored lowfat yogurt
  Ground nutmeg or cinnamon
  Condiments (suggestions follow), optional

In a 1- to 2-quart pan, bring water to a boil—1⅓ cups water if using white rice, 1⅔ cups if using brown rice. Add rice; return to a boil. Then reduce heat, cover, and simmer until rice is tender to bite (about 20 minutes for white rice, 45 minutes for brown rice).

In a bowl, lightly beat together eggs, sugar, vanilla, milk, and yogurt until blended. Stir in cooked rice. Pour into a shallow 1-quart casserole or soufflé dish and sprinkle with nutmeg.

Set a baking pan (a little larger than casserole or dish) on center rack of a 350° oven. Place casserole or dish in pan, then pour boiling water into pan to a depth of 1 to 1½ inches. Bake until pudding jiggles only slightly in center when casserole or dish is gently shaken (30 to 40 minutes for a casserole, 50 to 60 minutes for a soufflé dish). Let pudding cool until no longer hot, but still warm. If desired, offer condiments to sprinkle over individual servings. Makes 6 servings.

Condiments. Choose at least 3 of the following (offer about ½ cup of *each* condiment you choose): **granola-type cereal,** chopped **nuts, raisins,** chopped **dried apricots,** chopped **pitted dates,** and **unsweetened shredded coconut.**

Per serving: 6 grams protein, 39 grams carbohydrates, 3 grams total fat, 96 milligrams cholesterol, 66 milligrams sodium.

Lemon Meringue Rice Pudding

Preparation time: 20 to 30 minutes
Baking time: about 50 minutes

Calories per serving: 241

Imaginative cooks enjoy adding their own touches to everything they make—and simple desserts like rice pudding offer plenty of opportunity for embellishment. In this case, the pudding is enlivened with lemon and crowned with almond-studded meringue.

- ½ **cup firmly packed brown sugar**
- 1 **tablespoon cornstarch**
- ½ **teaspoon ground cinnamon**
- 3 **cups lowfat milk**
- 3 **cups cooked brown or white long-grain rice**
- 2 **tablespoons butter or margarine**
- 3 **eggs, separated**
- 1½ **teaspoons grated lemon peel**
- 6 **tablespoons lemon juice**
- ⅛ **teaspoon salt**
- ¼ **cup granulated sugar**
- ½ **teaspoon vanilla**
  About ⅓ cup sliced or slivered almonds

In a heavy 3-quart pan, stir together brown sugar, cornstarch, and cinnamon. Add ½ cup of the milk and stir until sugar is dissolved. In a small pan, scald remaining 2½ cups milk; stir into sugar mixture along with rice and butter. Place over medium-low heat and cook, stirring often, until steaming hot.

In a bowl, lightly beat egg yolks; stir about ½ cup of the hot rice mixture into yolks, then stir yolk mixture back into pan and mix well. Pour into a well-buttered shallow 2½-quart baking dish.

Bake, uncovered, in a 325° oven for 20 minutes. Stir in lemon peel and lemon juice; continue to bake until thick and creamy (about 20 more minutes). Remove from oven; increase oven temperature to 400°.

In small bowl of an electric mixer, beat egg whites and salt until foamy. Beat in granulated sugar, 1 tablespoon at a time, beating for about 30 seconds after each addition. Scrape down sides of bowl and continue to beat until sugar is completely dissolved. Beat in vanilla.

Spoon meringue over center of pudding and sprinkle with almonds. Bake, uncovered, until top is browned (about 10 minutes). Serve warm. Makes 10 servings.

Per serving: 7 grams protein, 36 grams carbohydrates, 8 grams total fat, 94 milligrams cholesterol, 114 milligrams sodium.

Orange Creams with Cherry Sauce

(Pictured on facing page)
Preparation time: 30 to 40 minutes
Chilling time: about 4 hours

Calories per serving: 179

Contrasts in color, flavor, and temperature make this dessert something special. Cool, delicate molded creams—one for each diner—are served with a warm sauce made from plump cherries and orange-flavored liqueur.

- 1 **envelope unflavored gelatin**
- ¼ **cup cold water**
- 3 **eggs**
- ⅓ **cup sugar**
- ¼ **cup orange-flavored liqueur**
- ½ **teaspoon vanilla**
- 1 **cup whipping cream**
  Cherry Sauce (recipe follows)
  Mint sprigs (optional)

In a 1- to 1½-quart pan, sprinkle gelatin over cold water; let stand for about 5 minutes to soften. Then stir over medium heat until gelatin is completely dissolved and mixture begins to simmer. Remove from heat.

In small bowl of an electric mixer, beat eggs and sugar on high speed until thick. Beat in gelatin mixture, liqueur, and vanilla.

In large bowl of mixer, beat cream until it holds soft peaks. Fold in egg mixture. Spoon evenly into 10 individual 4-ounce metal molds. Cover and refrigerate until firm (about 4 hours) or for up to 2 days.

To serve, prepare Cherry Sauce and keep warm. Then unmold orange creams: dip each mold to rim in hottest tap water just until edges liquefy slightly (about 20 seconds). Invert 1 mold on each dessert plate and shake firmly to dislodge; lift off mold. Spoon warm sauce alongside and over each serving; garnish with mint, if desired. Makes 10 servings.

Cherry Sauce. Thaw 1 package (16 oz.) **frozen unsweetened cherries.**

In a 1- to 2-quart pan, blend 2 tablespoons **sugar** and 1 tablespoon **cornstarch;** stir in ¼ cup **orange-flavored liqueur** and undrained cherries. Cook over medium-high heat, stirring gently, until mixture boils and thickens. Serve warm. If made ahead, let stand at room temperature for up to 4 hours (reheat before serving).

Per serving: 3 grams protein, 19 grams carbohydrates, 9 grams total fat, 109 milligrams cholesterol, 30 milligrams sodium.

Orange Creams with Cherry Sauce (recipe on facing page) offer pleasing contrasts.
The cool molded orange creams are a perfect foil for warm,
ruby-red cherry sauce accented with orange-flavored liqueur.

· ·

Ice Creams, Sherbets, Sorbets & Ices

REFRESHING FROZEN DELIGHTS

Cool, creamy, smooth, and delicious . . . ice cream is everyone's favorite. And sherbets, sorbets, and ices are almost as popular. These frosty treats are perfect after hot-weather meals, when you need a make-ahead dessert, or just about any time at all. If made with lean ingredients—lowfat milk, yogurt, buttermilk, fruit—they're even more appealing.

Our selection of light and luscious frozen desserts ranges from the familiar to the exotic. Vanilla Ice Milk, Pineapple Sherbet, and Strawberry Ice will please traditionalists; more adventurous cooks will want to try Cabernet Sauvignon Ice, Tropical Sorbet, or Frozen Tarragon Mousse with Strawberries.

Fresh Banana Gelato

Preparation time: 45 to 60 minutes
Freezing time: depends on the ice cream maker; see manufacturer's directions

Calories per serving: 145

Italians have a way with ice cream. Their smooth *gelato*—not as rich as typical American ice cream, but more intense in flavor—has been a favorite discovery of countless travelers to Italy. Our basic gelato is flavored with lemon and ripe bananas; we also include a variation made with bananas, fresh pineapple, and orange.

    Gelato Base (recipe follows)
 3 **medium-size ripe bananas**
 3 **tablespoons lemon juice**

Prepare Gelato Base and let cool.

Smoothly mash or purée bananas; place in a large bowl and stir in lemon juice. Stir 1 cup of the cooled Gelato Base into banana mixture until well blended; then gradually stir in remaining base. Pour into an ice- and salt-cooled or self-refrigerated ice cream maker; freeze according to manufacturer's directions. Gelato is ready to serve when frozen soft. For a firmer texture, repack with 1 part salt to 8 parts ice and let stand for 1 to 2 hours; or cover container of self-refrigerated machine and place in freezer for 1 to 2 hours. For best flavor and texture, serve gelato within 1 month.

To serve hard-frozen gelato, let stand at room temperature until slightly softened (about 10 minutes) before scooping. Makes 12 servings (about 1½ quarts *total*).

Gelato Base. In a 3- to 4-quart pan, combine 3 cups **whole milk**, ¾ cup **sugar**, 3 strips **lemon peel** (*each* about ½ by 2 inches, yellow part only), and a 2- to 3-inch section of **vanilla bean.** (Or use 1 teaspoon vanilla, adding it later, as directed.) Stir over medium heat just until sugar is dissolved.

Place 6 **egg yolks** in a medium-size bowl; beat until blended, then gradually beat 1 cup of the warm milk mixture into egg yolks. Pour egg yolk mixture into pan, beating constantly. Continue to cook, stirring, until custard coats the back of a metal spoon in a thin, velvety layer (about 10 minutes). *Do not bring mixture to scalding or custard will curdle.*

Pour custard through a fine wire strainer into a large bowl; discard lemon peel. Rinse vanilla bean, let dry, and reserve for later use. If using vanilla, stir in at this point. Let Gelato Base cool to room temperature.

Per serving: 4 grams protein, 22 grams carbohydrates, 5 grams total fat, 145 milligrams cholesterol, 35 milligrams sodium.

Tropical Fruit Gelato

Prepare **Gelato Base** as directed for **Fresh Banana Gelato.**

In a blender or food processor, combine 2 cups **fresh pineapple chunks;** 2 small ripe **bananas,** cut into chunks; 1 teaspoon grated **orange peel;** and 3 tablespoons **orange juice.** Whirl until puréed. Stir into cooled Gelato Base. Freeze and serve as directed for **Fresh Banana Gelato.**

Lemon Buttermilk Ice Cream

(Pictured on page 70)
Preparation time: 20 to 25 minutes
Freezing time: depends on the ice cream maker; see manufacturer's directions

Calories per serving: 104

Buttermilk is the base for this lemony dessert, helping to minimize calories and fat—and imparting a delightful tangy flavor.

 4 **eggs, separated**
 1½ **cups whipping cream**
 1 **cup sugar**
 3 **cups buttermilk**
 ¼ **cup lemon juice**
 3 **tablespoons grated lemon peel**
 1 **tablespoon vanilla**
    Quartered lemon slices and shredded lemon peel (optional)

In small bowl of an electric mixer, beat egg whites until they hold stiff peaks; set aside.

In large bowl of mixer, beat cream until it holds soft peaks; beat in egg yolks, sugar, buttermilk, lemon juice, grated lemon peel, and vanilla. Fold in egg whites.

Pour mixture into a 1-gallon ice- and salt-cooled or self-refrigerated ice cream maker; freeze according to manufacturer's directions, using 1 part salt to 8 parts ice. Ice cream is ready to serve when frozen soft. For a firmer texture, repack with 1 part salt to 4 parts ice and let stand for 1 to 2 hours; or cover container of self-refrigerated machine and place in freezer for 1 to 2 hours.

To serve hard-frozen ice cream, let stand at room temperature until slightly softened before scooping. Garnish each serving with lemon slices and shredded lemon peel, if desired. Makes 24 servings (about 3 quarts *total*).

Per serving: 2 grams protein, 11 grams carbohydrates, 6 grams total fat, 63 milligrams cholesterol, 49 milligrams sodium.

A dish of Lemon Buttermilk Ice Cream (recipe on page 69) tastes as cool and refreshing
as it looks—and at only 104 calories, who could turn it down?
The buttermilk keeps it low in fat and lends a delightful tanginess.

. . . .

Vanilla Tofulato

Preparation time: 15 to 20 minutes
Freezing time: depends on the ice cream maker; see manufacturer's directions

Calories per serving of Vanilla Tofulato: 160

What's the result when Oriental tofu meets Italian gelato? A smooth and flavorful frozen dessert we call "tofulato." Inexpensive tofu (bean curd) is low in fat and calories and takes well to a variety of flavorings—ginger, malt, even jalapeño chiles. (If you like the idea of using tofu in desserts, you might also try Tofu Banana-Pineapple Cheesecake, page 15.)

Once soft, tofulato melts quickly. To keep it firmer longer, include the small amount of unflavored gelatin we suggest.

> 2 teaspoons unflavored gelatin (optional)
> ⅓ cup water (optional)
> ⅔ cup sugar
> 1 package (1 lb.) soft tofu (bean curd), drained (2 cups)
> 1½ cups buttermilk, plain lowfat yogurt, whole milk, or whipping cream
> ⅓ cup whipping cream
> 2 teaspoons vanilla
> Additional flavoring (choices and directions follow), optional

If using gelatin, in a small pan, sprinkle gelatin over water and let stand for about 5 minutes to soften. Stir in sugar; then stir over medium heat until gelatin is completely dissolved.

In a food processor or blender, combine tofu and gelatin-sugar mixture (or just sugar, if not using gelatin). Whirl until smooth. Stir tofu mixture into buttermilk; stir in the ⅓ cup whipping cream, vanilla, and, if desired, additional flavoring.

Pour into an ice- and salt-cooled or self-refrigerated ice cream maker; freeze according to manufacturer's directions. Tofulato is ready to serve when frozen soft. For a firmer texture, repack with 1 part salt to 4 parts ice and let stand for 1 to 2 hours; or cover container of self-refrigerated machine and set in freezer for 1 to 2 hours. For best flavor and texture, serve tofulato within 3 weeks.

To serve hard-frozen tofulato, let stand at room temperature until slightly softened (about 30 minutes) before scooping. Makes 8 servings (about 1 quart *total*).

Additional flavoring. Our basic Vanilla Tofulato can be flavored in many ways; choose from the following. Variations made without dairy products yield only 2½ to 3 cups.

Nondairy vanilla. Prepare **Vanilla Tofulato,** but omit all dairy products.

Banana. Prepare **Vanilla Tofulato,** using buttermilk or yogurt and the ⅓ cup whipping cream; stir in ⅓ cup mashed ripe **banana** until well blended.

Ginger or ginger-banana. Prepare **Vanilla Tofulato,** using buttermilk or yogurt and the ⅓ cup whipping cream; stir in ⅓ cup chopped **crystallized ginger** and (for ginger-banana flavor) ⅓ cup mashed ripe **banana** until well blended.

Malt or malt-banana. Prepare **Vanilla Tofulato,** using milk and the ⅓ cup whipping cream (if using banana, you may omit all dairy products). Whirl ½ cup **unflavored malted milk powder** and (for malt-banana flavor) ⅓ cup mashed ripe **banana** into sugar-tofu mixture until well blended.

Chocolate malt. Melt 1 package (6 oz.) **semisweet chocolate chips** or 1 cup chopped semisweet chocolate in a small frying pan over lowest heat, stirring constantly. Set aside. Prepare **Vanilla Tofulato** with malt or malt-banana flavoring (see above); whirl melted chocolate into sugar-tofu mixture until well blended.

Carob. Melt ½ cup chopped **carob** in a small frying pan over low heat, stirring constantly. Set aside. Prepare **Vanilla Tofulato,** using milk and the ⅓ cup whipping cream (or omit all dairy products); whirl melted carob into sugar-tofu mixture until well blended.

Chilly chile. Beat ½ cup **red, green, or yellow jalapeño jelly** until smooth. Prepare **Vanilla Tofulato,** using buttermilk or yogurt and the ⅓ cup whipping cream; whirl jelly into sugar-tofu mixture until well blended.

Hazelnut praline. Prepare ½ recipe **Praline Powder** in a 10- to 12-inch frying pan as directed on page 41, using 1 cup **sugar** and ½ cup **hazelnuts** (filberts). Prepare **Vanilla Tofulato,** using milk and the ⅓ cup whipping cream (or omit all dairy products); stir in Praline Powder until well blended.

Fresh berry. In a blender or food processor, purée 1½ cups **berries** (strawberries, raspberries, olallieberries, boysenberries, or blueberries) with 3 tablespoons **sugar;** if desired, rub purée through a wire strainer and discard seeds. In a 2- to 3-quart pan, bring purée to a boil; reduce heat and boil gently, uncovered, until fruit is reduced to ½ cup (about 20 minutes), stirring often. Stir in 2 teaspoons **lemon juice.** Prepare **Vanilla Tofulato,** using buttermilk or yogurt and the ⅓ cup whipping cream; stir in berry purée until well blended.

Per serving of Vanilla Tofulato: 7 grams protein, 20 grams carbohydrates, 6 grams total fat, 13 milligrams cholesterol, 55 milligrams sodium.

Vanilla Frozen Yogurt

(Pictured on page 83)

Preparation time: 25 to 30 minutes
Freezing time: depends on the ice cream maker; see manufacturer's directions

Calories per serving: 135

Ice cream without the guilt—that's how many frozen yogurt devotees view their chosen dessert. Though creamy, cool, and delicious, it's low in fat and high in protein. The basic recipe below makes a vanilla-flavored dessert; for fruit-flavored yogurt, prepare one of the variations.

> 1 **envelope unflavored gelatin**
> ½ **cup whole milk**
> 2 **whole eggs or 2 egg whites**
> 3 **cups plain lowfat yogurt**
> ¾ **cup sugar; or ⅓ cup honey and ¼ cup sugar**
> 2 **tablespoons vanilla**

In a small pan, sprinkle gelatin over milk; let stand for about 5 minutes to soften. Then stir over medium heat until gelatin is completely dissolved. Let cool for about 5 minutes.

If using whole eggs, separate eggs. Set whites aside in a medium-size bowl. Place egg yolks in a large bowl and beat lightly with a wire whisk. Beat in yogurt and ½ cup of the sugar (or the ⅓ cup honey) until smoothly blended. Beat in gelatin mixture and vanilla.

Beat egg whites until they hold soft peaks; gradually add remaining ¼ cup sugar, beating until mixture holds stiff, glossy peaks. Fold meringue into yogurt mixture.

Pour into a 2-quart or larger ice- and salt-cooled or self-refrigerated ice cream maker. Freeze according to manufacturer's directions. Yogurt is ready to serve when frozen soft. For a firmer texture, repack with ice and salt according to manufacturer's directions and let stand for 1 to 2 hours; or cover container of self-refrigerated machine and place in freezer for 1 to 2 hours.

To serve hard-frozen yogurt, let stand at room temperature until softened (about 30 minutes) before scooping. Makes 10 servings (about 5 cups *total*).

Per serving: 6 grams protein, 21 grams carbohydrates, 3 grams total fat, 61 milligrams cholesterol, 68 milligrams sodium.

Fresh Berry Frozen Yogurt

Place about 2 cups hulled **strawberries**, raspberries, or olallieberries in a large bowl; mash well. (Or whirl in a blender or food processor until coarsely crushed.) You should have 1½ cups. Add ½ cup **sugar;** let stand until juices form. Spoon off and reserve ½ cup of the juice.

Follow directions for **Vanilla Frozen Yogurt,** but omit milk and use the ½ cup berry juice to dissolve gelatin. Omit the ½ cup sugar (or ⅓ cup honey) and vanilla from yogurt mixture; add 2 tablespoons **lemon juice,** sweetened berries, and any remaining juices to yogurt mixture before folding in meringue. Makes 16 servings.

Fresh Peach, Nectarine, or Apricot Frozen Yogurt

Remove and discard pits from peeled ripe **peaches** or unpeeled nectarines or apricots. In a blender or food processor, whirl fruit until coarsely puréed; you need 1½ cups. Add ½ cup **sugar** and 2 tablespoons **lemon juice;** let stand until juices form. Spoon off and reserve ½ cup of the juice.

Follow directions for **Vanilla Frozen Yogurt,** but omit milk and use the ½ cup fruit juice to dissolve gelatin. Omit the ½ cup sugar (or ⅓ cup honey) and vanilla from yogurt mixture; add sweetened fruit, any remaining juices, and ⅛ teaspoon **almond extract** to yogurt mixture. After folding in meringue, taste; then add up to ¼ cup more **sugar,** if desired. Makes 16 servings.

Banana-Lime Frozen Yogurt

Follow directions for **Vanilla Frozen Yogurt,** but omit milk and use 1 can (6 oz.) **frozen limeade or lemonade concentrate** (thawed) to dissolve gelatin. Omit vanilla and add 1 cup mashed ripe **bananas** (about 2 large bananas) and ⅓ cup **dark rum** (optional) to yogurt mixture. When mixture is frozen soft, stir in about ½ cup **sweetened flaked or shredded coconut.** Makes 16 servings.

Spiced Apple-Nut Frozen Yogurt

Follow directions for **Vanilla Frozen Yogurt,** but omit milk and use 1 can (6 oz.) **frozen apple juice concentrate** (thawed) to dissolve gelatin. Substitute about ½ cup firmly packed **brown sugar** for granulated sugar (or granulated sugar plus honey); stir ¼ cup of the brown sugar into yogurt mixture and beat ¼ cup into egg whites. Add more brown sugar after folding meringue into yogurt mixture, if desired. Substitute ¼ teaspoon *each* **ground cloves** and **ground nutmeg** for vanilla. When mixture is frozen soft, stir in about ½ cup chopped **almonds** or walnuts. Makes 10 servings.

Frozen Yogurt Pops

Preparation time: 5 to 10 minutes
Freezing time: about 3½ hours total

Calories per pop: 60

Let the children help prepare these easy-to-make yogurt pops. They'll love matching up different flavors of yogurt and fruit juice and inserting the wooden sticks into the partially frozen yogurt mixture. When the pops are firm, it's easy to peel off the paper and enjoy a nutritious snack or dessert.

  1 **can (6 oz.) frozen orange, grape, or apple juice concentrate**
  ¾ **cup water**
  1 **cup plain or fruit-flavored lowfat yogurt**

In a blender or food processor, whirl juice concentrate, water, and yogurt until well blended. Divide mixture equally among eight 3-ounce paper drinking cups. Cover cups and set in freezer until partially frozen (about 1½ hours), then insert a wooden stick in each cup. Freeze until firm (about 2 hours). Makes 8 pops.

Per pop: 2 grams protein, 12 grams carbohydrates, .48 gram total fat, 2 milligrams cholesterol, 21 milligrams sodium.

Vanilla Ice Milk

Preparation time: 10 to 15 minutes
Freezing time: about 3½ hours total

Calories per serving: 163

You don't need an ice cream maker to prepare this refreshing ice milk. If you prefer a richer flavor and don't mind the extra calories, add 1 cup of whipping cream along with the milk.

  3 **eggs**
  ¾ **cup sugar**
  ½ **cup light corn syrup**
 1½ **tablespoons vanilla**
  ⅛ **teaspoon salt**
  4 **cups whole milk**

In a large bowl, beat eggs with a rotary beater until well blended. Stir in sugar; continue to beat until mixture is thick and lemon-colored. Mix in corn syrup, vanilla, and salt; continue to beat until well blended. Stir in milk.

Pour mixture into an 8- or 9-inch square metal pan. Cover and freeze until a 2-inch border around edges is frozen solid (about 1½ hours). Break

partially frozen ice milk into chunks with a heavy spoon; pour into large bowl of an electric mixer and beat until fluffy. Cover airtight; return to freezer and freeze until firm (about 2 hours).

To serve, let ice milk stand at room temperature until slightly softened before scooping. Makes 12 servings (about 2 quarts *total*).

Per serving: 4 grams protein, 27 grams carbohydrates, 4 grams total fat, 80 milligrams cholesterol, 90 milligrams sodium.

Peach Tortoni

Preparation time: 40 to 50 minutes
Freezing time: about 6 hours

Calories per serving: 143

Peaches and cream taste so good together that inventive cooks are always coming up with new ways to present them. In these individual-size frozen desserts, diced peaches in a fluffy meringue fill an almond macaroon crust.

 1½ **cups coarsely crushed almond macaroon cookies**
  ¾ **cup peach jam**
  1 **cup peeled, coarsely chopped ripe peaches**
  ½ **cup sugar**
  1 **egg white**
 1½ **teaspoons lemon juice**
  ½ **teaspoon vanilla**
  ¼ **cup whipping cream**
     About ¼ cup sliced almonds

Line 18 muffin cups with paper baking cups. In a small bowl, mix crushed cookies and jam; divide mixture evenly among muffin cups, pressing mixture to cover bottoms of cups. Set aside.

In large bowl of an electric mixer, combine peaches, sugar, egg white, lemon juice, and vanilla. Beat on low speed to blend; then beat on high speed until mixture holds stiff peaks (about 7 minutes). In small bowl of mixer, beat cream until it holds very soft peaks; fold whipped cream into peach meringue.

Mound mixture equally in crumb-lined cups. Top each cup with a few almond slices. Freeze until solid (about 6 hours). Serve; or wrap airtight and store in freezer for up to 2 weeks. Let stand at room temperature for about 5 minutes before serving. Makes 18 servings.

Per serving: 1 gram protein, 25 grams carbohydrates, 5 grams total fat, 17 milligrams cholesterol, 10 milligrams sodium.

Frozen Tarragon Mousse with Strawberries

(Pictured on front cover and on facing page)
Preparation time: 1 to 1½ hours
Freezing time: at least 6 hours

Calories per serving: 199

Tarragon and strawberries for dessert? Handled with finesse, they make a great team. The sweet, aromatic tang of tarragon is emphasized in a frozen mousse made of wine, lemon, and eggs—a perfect complement to the berries' sweetness.

You can use either fresh or dry tarragon to make this dessert; if using the dry herb, steep it in the wine for half an hour to release its flavor.

- ¾ cup dry white wine
- 3 tablespoons chopped fresh tarragon or 1½ tablespoons dry tarragon
- 1 cup sugar
- 6 egg yolks
- ¼ teaspoon grated lemon peel
- 1 tablespoon lemon juice
- 1 cup whipping cream
  About 2 cups strawberries
  Sugar
  Shredded lemon peel (optional)

Combine wine and tarragon in a 1- to 2-quart pan. (If using dry tarragon, heat to steaming; let stand for 30 minutes.) Add the 1 cup sugar, bring to a boil, and boil gently until syrup registers 220°F on a candy thermometer.

Place egg yolks in the top of a double boiler. Gradually pour hot syrup into yolks, beating constantly with a portable electric mixer or rotary beater. Set over simmering water and continue to beat until mixture holds soft peaks (about 10 minutes). Remove from heat. Set over cold water and continue to beat until cool. Stir in grated lemon peel and lemon juice.

In a medium-size bowl, beat cream until it holds stiff peaks; fold into egg yolk mixture just until blended. Cover airtight and freeze until firm (at least 6 hours) or for up to 1 month.

To serve, reserve 10 whole, unhulled strawberries for garnish; if desired, make 5 or 6 lengthwise cuts in each reserved berry, then gently spread berry slightly so it resembles a fan. Hull and slice remaining strawberries and sweeten to taste with sugar. Serve small scoops of mousse with sliced strawberries; garnish each serving with a whole strawberry and, if desired, shredded lemon peel. Makes 10 servings.

Per serving: 3 grams protein, 24 grams carbohydrates, 11 grams total fat, 190 milligrams cholesterol, 15 milligrams sodium.

Orange-Banana Sherbet

Preparation time: 30 to 45 minutes
Freezing time: about 6 hours total

Calories per serving: 102

For those who like to serve desserts made without sugar, these sherbets—one sweetened with concentrated orange juice, the other with dates—will be a welcome find. Bananas and yogurt lend smooth texture and rich flavor to both desserts.

- 2 large ripe bananas, cut into chunks
- 1 can (6 oz.) frozen orange juice concentrate, partially thawed
- 1 cup plain lowfat yogurt
- ½ cup fruity white wine (such as French Colombard or Chenin Blanc); or 1½ tablespoons lemon juice plus enough water to make ½ cup liquid

In a food processor or blender, combine bananas and orange juice concentrate; whirl until smooth. Add yogurt and wine and whirl until well blended. Pour into an 8- or 9-inch square metal pan, cover, and freeze until solid (about 4 hours).

Let sherbet stand at room temperature until you can break it into chunks with a heavy spoon. In a food processor, whirl chunks, a portion at a time; use on-off pulses at first to break up chunks, then whirl continuously until smooth and slushy. (Or place all chunks in large bowl of an electric mixer and beat until smooth and slushy, increasing mixer speed from low to high as sherbet softens.)

Serve at once; or return to metal pan, cover airtight, and freeze until firm (about 2 hours). To serve hard-frozen sherbet, let stand at room temperature until slightly softened (about 10 minutes) before scooping. Makes 8 servings (about 1 quart *total*).

Per serving: 2 grams protein, 20 grams carbohydrates, .63 gram total fat, 2 milligrams cholesterol, 22 milligrams sodium.

Date Sherbet

Coarsely chop ¾ cup **pitted dates;** place in a food processor or blender. Add 1 cup **fruity white wine,** such as French Colombard or Chenin Blanc (or use 3 tablespoons lemon juice plus enough apple juice or water to make 1 cup liquid). Whirl until dates are finely chopped. Add 2 large ripe **bananas,** cut into chunks; 1 cup **plain lowfat yogurt;** and ¼ teaspoon **ground nutmeg.** Whirl until smooth.

Freeze, beat, and serve sherbet as directed for **Orange-Banana Sherbet.**

A touch of tarragon adds an interesting flavor accent to sophisticated
Frozen Tarragon Mousse with Strawberries (recipe on facing page).
The sweet, creamy mousse is served in small scoops over sliced berries.

. . . .

Creamy Raspberry Sherbet

Preparation time: 10 to 15 minutes
Freezing time: about 3 hours

Calories per serving: 62

Juicy, sweet-tart fresh raspberries are showcased in this simple sherbet: it contains only berries, milk, and a little sugar. You freeze the milk in an ice cube tray, then use a food processor to blend the milk cubes with the chilled or frozen fruit. In moments, the sherbet is ready to eat.

If you don't have a food processor, you can use an electric mixer and a blender. The sherbet may be coarser and softer, though, and you may need to freeze it until it firms up.

> 1 cup whole milk
> 1 cup raspberries
> 4 to 6 tablespoons sugar

Pour milk into a divided ice cube tray; freeze until solid (about 3 hours). Refrigerate berries until very cold (or freeze them).

Shortly before serving, remove frozen milk and berries (if frozen) from freezer. Let stand for about 5 minutes at room temperature. Remove milk cubes from tray; if cubes are large, cut them into small chunks. In a food processor, whirl milk chunks, a portion at a time; use on-off pulses at first to break up chunks, then whirl continuously until velvety. With motor running, drop in berries (about ⅓ at a time) and sugar; whirl until smooth, then serve.

If you don't have a food processor, place all frozen milk in large bowl of an electric mixer and break into small pieces with a heavy spoon. Then beat until smooth, increasing mixer speed from low to high as ice softens. Set aside. Purée berries in a blender, adding 2 to 4 tablespoons milk to start blender, if needed. Beat fruit purée into milk slush. Stir in sugar. For a soft sherbet, serve immediately. If texture is too soft, cover mixture and freeze until it reaches desired firmness—or serve as a slushy shake.

Store any leftover sherbet in an airtight container in the freezer; let hard-frozen sherbet stand at room temperature until softened (15 to 30 minutes) before scooping. Makes 6 servings (about 3 cups *total*).

Per serving: 1 gram protein, 13 grams carbohydrates, 1 gram total fat, 4 milligrams cholesterol, 15 milligrams sodium.

Creamy Plum Sherbet

Follow directions for **Creamy Raspberry Sherbet,** but substitute 1 cup diced **purple plums,** such as Satsuma or Nubiana (3 or 4 plums), for raspberries.

Creamy Peach Sherbet

Follow directions for **Creamy Raspberry Sherbet,** but substitute 1 cup peeled, diced ripe **peaches** (in ½-inch chunks) for raspberries.

Creamy Cantaloupe Sherbet

Follow directions for **Creamy Raspberry Sherbet,** but substitute 1 cup peeled, seeded, diced ripe **cantaloupe** (in ½-inch chunks) for raspberries. Also add 1½ tablespoons **orange juice** and reduce sugar to 2 to 3 tablespoons.

Pineapple Sherbet

Preparation time: 30 to 45 minutes
Freezing time: about 3½ hours total

Calories per serving: 90

Crushed pineapple and buttermilk flavor this tangy sherbet. Meringue, folded in when the sherbet is partially frozen, gives the dessert its light texture.

> 2 eggs, separated
> ¾ cup sugar
> 1 can (about 8 oz.) crushed pineapple packed in its own juice
> 2 tablespoons lemon juice
> 2 cups buttermilk
> 1 teaspoon unflavored gelatin
> 1 tablespoon water

In a blender, combine egg yolks, ½ cup of the sugar, pineapple and its juice, lemon juice, and buttermilk. Whirl until blended. Set aside.

In a small bowl, sprinkle gelatin over water. Let stand for about 5 minutes to soften, then set over hot water and stir until gelatin is completely dissolved. Blend gelatin into buttermilk mixture; pour mixture into an 8- or 9-inch square metal pan, cover, and freeze until firm around edges (about 1½ hours).

In a medium-size bowl, beat egg whites until they hold soft, moist peaks; gradually add remaining ¼ cup sugar, beating until mixture holds stiff peaks. Set aside.

Break partially frozen sherbet into chunks with a heavy spoon. Pour into large bowl of an electric mixer; beat until fluffy. Fold in egg white mixture. Cover airtight and freeze until solid (about 2 hours). To serve hard-frozen sherbet, let stand at room temperature until slightly softened before scooping. Makes 12 servings (about 1½ quarts *total*).

Per serving: 3 grams protein, 18 grams carbohydrates, 1 gram total fat, 47 milligrams cholesterol, 55 milligrams sodium.

Champagne-Cinnamon Snowball Sherbet

Preparation time: 40 to 50 minutes
Chilling time: about 1½ hours
Freezing time: at least 12 hours

Calories per serving: 164

White as snow, this frosty sherbet takes its pale coolness from a spiced champagne syrup blended and frozen with an airy meringue. It's delightful alone, sparkling and dressy when served with a splash of champagne.

It's best to make this sherbet a day ahead to give it ample time to freeze.

- ½ cup sugar
- 1 cup water
- 2 cinnamon sticks (*each* about 3 inches long)
- 2 tablespoons lemon juice
- At least 2 cups champagne or other dry to sweet white sparkling wine
- Italian Meringue (recipe follows)
- 6 additional cinnamon sticks (*each* about 3 inches long), optional

In a 1- to 2-quart pan, combine sugar, water, and the 2 cinnamon sticks. Bring to a boil over high heat; continue to boil, uncovered, until syrup registers 210°F on a candy thermometer (about 5 minutes). Remove from heat and stir in lemon juice and 2 cups of the champagne. Refrigerate until cold (1½ to 2 hours). Then pour syrup through a wire strainer into an 8- or 9-inch square metal pan. Rinse cinnamon sticks and let dry; reserve for garnish, if desired.

Cover champagne mixture and freeze until softly but evenly frozen (at least 8 hours). Meanwhile, prepare Italian Meringue.

With a heavy spoon, break up champagne mixture and stir until slushy. Fold mixture into meringue until well blended. Cover airtight and freeze until firm (at least 4 hours); after 2 to 3 hours, fold mixture occasionally to keep it evenly blended as it hardens, or it will separate into layers. For best flavor and texture, serve sherbet within 3 months.

To serve, use an ice cream scoop to shape about ½ cup of sherbet at a time into a ball. For each serving, place 2 of these snowballs in an 8-ounce stemmed glass or dish. If desired, carefully pour additional champagne over snowballs to fill glasses

partially. Garnish each serving with a cinnamon stick, if desired. Makes 8 servings (about 2 quarts *total*).

Italian Meringue. In a 1- to 2-quart pan, stir together 1 cup **sugar** and ½ cup **water.** Bring to a boil over medium-high heat; continue to boil, uncovered, until syrup registers 228°F on a candy thermometer (about 5 minutes).

Meanwhile, in large bowl of an electric mixer, beat 4 **egg whites** until they hold soft peaks. Beating constantly, slowly pour hot syrup into egg whites in a thin, steady stream (avoid beaters); continue to beat until mixture holds stiff, glossy peaks. Cover and refrigerate until cold (at least 1 hour) or until next day.

Per serving: 2 grams protein, 41 grams carbohydrates, .02 gram total fat, 0 milligram cholesterol, 29 milligrams sodium.

Champagne-Allspice Snowball Sherbet

Follow directions for **Champagne-Cinnamon Snowball Sherbet,** but substitute 1 teaspoon **whole allspice,** coarsely crushed, for the 2 cinnamon sticks.

Champagne-Cardamom Snowball Sherbet

Remove seeds from 2 teaspoons **cardamom pods;** coarsely crush seeds. Follow directions for **Champagne-Cinnamon Snowball Sherbet,** but substitute the crushed cardamom for the 2 cinnamon sticks.

Champagne-Clove Snowball Sherbet

Follow directions for **Champagne-Cinnamon Snowball Sherbet,** but substitute 2 teaspoons **whole cloves** for the 2 cinnamon sticks.

Champagne-Ginger Snowball Sherbet

Follow directions for **Champagne-Cinnamon Snowball Sherbet,** but substitute 2 tablespoons slivered **fresh ginger** for the 2 cinnamon sticks (peel ginger, if desired).

Champagne-Nutmeg Snowball Sherbet

Follow directions for **Champagne-Cinnamon Snowball Sherbet,** but substitute 1 teaspoon **ground nutmeg** for the 2 cinnamon sticks; do not strain spice syrup.

Nestled in a snowy Meringue Shell (page 16), a scoop of Buttermilk Fruit Sherbet (recipe on facing page)—here, made with boysenberries—is a pretty picture.
Top it off with a drizzle of Blueberry Sauce (page 40) for a memorable dessert.

. . . .

Buttermilk Fruit Sherbet

(Pictured on facing page)

Preparation time: 25 to 35 minutes
Freezing time: depends on the ice cream maker; see manufacturer's instructions

Calories per serving of Buttermilk Berry Sherbet: 129

You can get as exotic as you like when making our tart buttermilk sherbet—we offer several different fruit variations, from berry to melon to papaya. Unlike most sweet, icy purchased sherbets, these homemade ones taste as creamy and rich as ice cream.

>   Fruit purée (choices and directions follow)
> 2 **eggs**
> ½ **teaspoon salt**
> 2 **cups sugar**
> 4 **cups buttermilk**

Prepare fruit purée of your choice; set aside.

Separate eggs. Set whites aside in a 3-quart or larger bowl. In a 2½-quart or larger bowl, combine egg yolks, salt, and ½ cup of the sugar; beat until thick and lemon-colored. Gradually add fruit purée and 1 cup more sugar; beat until sugar is dissolved. Blend in buttermilk.

Beat egg whites until they hold soft peaks; gradually add remaining ½ cup sugar and continue to beat until mixture holds stiff, moist peaks. Gradually fold buttermilk mixture into egg white mixture just until blended.

Pour into a 1-gallon or larger ice- and salt-cooled ice cream maker (it should be no more than ⅔ full). Freeze according to manufacturer's directions, using 1 part salt to about 3 parts ice.

Sherbet is ready to eat when frozen soft. For a firmer texture, repack with ice and salt according to manufacturer's directions and let stand for 1 to 2 hours. To serve hard-frozen sherbet, let stand at room temperature until slightly softened before scooping. Makes 20 servings (about 2½ quarts *total*).

Fruit purée. Choose from the following 4 purées.

Berry. In a blender or food processor, whirl 6 cups **fresh or thawed frozen unsweetened boysenberries,** blackberries, olallieberries, or raspberries until smooth (you should have 3 cups purée). Add 1 tablespoon *each* **lemon juice** and **vanilla** and 1 teaspoon grated **lemon peel;** stir to blend.

Cantaloupe. Peel and seed 2 small **cantaloupes** (about 3½ lbs. *total*). Cut fruit into chunks. Whirl in a blender or food processor until smooth (you should have 3½ cups purée). Add 2 tablespoons **lemon juice,** 1 teaspoon *each* **vanilla** and grated **lemon peel,** and ¼ teaspoon **ground ginger;** stir to blend.

Mango. Peel 4 medium-size ripe **mangoes;** slice fruit from pits. Whirl in a blender or food processor until smooth (you should have 3¼ cups purée). Add ¼ cup **orange juice,** 1 teaspoon grated **orange peel,** and 2 teaspoons *each* **lemon juice** and **vanilla;** stir to blend.

Papaya. Peel and seed about 4 medium-size **papayas;** cut into chunks. Whirl in a blender or food processor until smooth (you should have 3½ cups purée). Add ¼ cup **lime juice,** 1½ teaspoons **vanilla,** and 1 teaspoon grated **lemon or lime peel;** stir to blend.

Per serving of Buttermilk Berry Sherbet: 3 grams protein, 28 grams carbohydrates, 1 gram total fat, 29 milligrams cholesterol, 113 milligrams sodium.

Fresh Mint Sherbet

Preparation time: 30 to 40 minutes
Freezing time: about 7 hours total

Calories per serving: 105

Crushed fresh mint flavors this exceptionally cool, smooth sherbet. Garnish each serving with a mint sprig or a little shaved chocolate, if you like.

> 1 **cup water**
> 1 **cup sugar**
> 1 **cup lightly packed mint sprigs**
> ½ **cup lemon juice**
>   **Few drops of green food color**
> 2 **egg whites**

In a small pan, combine water and ¾ cup of the sugar. Bring to a boil; boil, uncovered, stirring constantly, until sugar is dissolved. In a large bowl, crush mint with a pastry blender or a wooden spoon. Pour hot syrup over mint; crush mint again. Cover and let cool. Stir in lemon juice and food color. Pour through a fine strainer into an 8- or 9-inch square metal pan; discard mint. Cover syrup in pan and freeze until slushy (at least 4 hours).

In small bowl of an electric mixer, beat egg whites until frothy; gradually add remaining ¼ cup sugar and continue to beat until mixture holds stiff, glossy peaks.

Spoon partially frozen sherbet into large bowl of mixer. Beat until smooth; fold in egg white mixture, blending gently but thoroughly. Return to metal pan, cover, and freeze until firm (at least 3 hours). Let hard-frozen sherbet stand at room temperature until slightly softened before scooping. Makes about 8 servings.

Per serving: .97 gram protein, 26 grams carbohydrates, .07 gram total fat, 0 milligram cholesterol, 16 milligrams sodium.

Sorbetto

Preparation time: 25 to 35 minutes
Freezing time: depends on the ice cream maker; see manufacturer's directions

Calories per serving of Berry Sorbetto: 184

Fruity sorbetto is the Italian version of sorbet. Like its cousin *gelato* (see page 69), it's distinguished by a delightful intensity of flavor. Depending on your preference, you can make our sorbetto with a purée of pineapple or berries, or with grape, orange, or lemon juice.

> **2 to 3 cups Sugar Syrup (recipe follows)**
> **Fruit purée or juice (choices and directions follow)**

Prepare Sugar Syrup and let cool.

Prepare purée or juice of your choice. Mix 2 cups of the syrup with berry or pineapple purée; or mix 2 to 3 cups of the syrup with fruit juice.

Pour mixture into an ice- and salt-cooled or self-refrigerated ice cream maker and freeze according to manufacturer's directions. Sorbetto is ready to serve when frozen soft. For a firmer texture, repack with ice and salt according to manufacturer's directions and let stand for 1 to 2 hours; or cover container of self-refrigerated machine and place in freezer for 1 to 2 hours. For best flavor and texture, serve sorbetto within 1 month.

To serve hard-frozen sorbetto, let stand at room temperature until slightly softened (about 10 minutes) before scooping. Makes 12 servings (about 1½ quarts *total*).

Sugar Syrup. In a 2- to 3-quart pan, combine 2½ cups *each* **sugar** and **water.** Bring to a boil over high heat; continue to boil, uncovered, for 5 minutes. Let cool. If made ahead, cover and refrigerate (syrup will keep indefinitely). Makes 3 cups.

Fruit purée. For a smoother texture, both pineapple and berry purées may be strained after preparation: force purée through a wire strainer, pressing firmly with a spoon. Discard pulp or seeds.

Berry. Whirl 6 cups hulled **strawberries,** raspberries, or olallieberries in a blender or food processor until puréed. Add ⅓ cup **lemon juice** to strawberry purée, 1 tablespoon lemon juice to raspberry or olallieberry purée. Strain, if desired. Use at once.

Pineapple. Whirl 4 cups **fresh pineapple chunks** and ¼ cup **lemon juice** in a blender or food processor until puréed. Strain, if desired. Use at once.

Fruit juice. Fruit juices make delicate-colored sorbetto. If you prefer a deeper hue, add a few drops of food color to the fruit juice.

Thompson seedless grape. Whirl 8 cups stemmed **Thompson seedless grapes** with ¼ cup **lemon juice** in a blender or food processor until puréed. Pour purée through a wire strainer; discard skins. Add 1 drop *each* **yellow food color** and **green food color,** if desired. Use at once.

Orange. Stir together 2 cups **orange juice** and ¼ cup **lemon juice;** add 1 drop *each* **yellow food color** and **red food color,** if desired. Use at once.

Lemon. Stir together 2 cups **lemon juice** and 2 cups **water;** add 1 drop **yellow food color,** if desired. Use at once.

Per serving of Berry Sorbetto: .48 gram protein, 47 grams carbohydrates, .29 gram total fat, 0 milligram cholesterol, 3 milligrams sodium.

Pear Sorbet

Preparation time: 40 to 50 minutes
Freezing time: about 6 hours total

Calories per serving: 130

Sorbets—frozen purées of fruit and sugar syrup—are sometimes served for a cooling break between courses of a meal. They also make an elegant light dessert. To finish a dinner in style, offer scoops of this icy pear sorbet in pretty stemware, topped with toasted almonds and ripe pear slices.

> **½ cup dry white wine**
> **1 tablespoon lemon juice**
> **⅓ cup sugar**
> **2 large firm-ripe pears, peeled, cored, and sliced**
> **¼ cup slivered almonds (optional)**
> **Firm-ripe pear slices (optional)**

In a small pan, combine wine, lemon juice, sugar, and the 2 sliced pears. Bring to a boil over high heat; then reduce heat, cover, and simmer until pears are tender when pierced (5 to 8 minutes). Pour fruit and syrup into a blender or food processor and whirl until puréed; pour into an 8- or 9-inch square metal pan, cover, and freeze until solid (4 to 5 hours).

Let sorbet stand at room temperature until you can break it into chunks with a heavy spoon. Whirl chunks in a food processor, a portion at a time; use on-off pulses at first to break up chunks, then whirl continuously until smooth and slushy. (Or place all chunks in large bowl of an electric mixer and beat until smooth and slushy, increasing mixer speed from low to high as sorbet softens.)

Pour sorbet into a freezer container; cover airtight and freeze until firm (about 2 hours). For best flavor and texture, serve within 2 months.

If using almonds, spread in a shallow baking pan and toast in a 350° oven until golden (about 8 minutes), stirring occasionally. Set aside to cool.

Let hard-frozen sorbet stand at room temperature until slightly softened before scooping into individual bowls. Garnish each serving with 1 tablespoon of the toasted almonds and a few pear slices, if desired. Makes 4 servings (about 2 cups *total*).

Per serving: .43 gram protein, 34 grams carbohydrates, .42 gram total fat, 0 milligram cholesterol, 2 milligrams sodium.

Tropical Sorbet

Preparation time: 30 to 40 minutes
Freezing time: about 3½ hours total

Calories per serving of Mango Sorbet: 179

Tropical fruits—some with unusual shapes and exotic flavors—are rapidly increasing in availability. They'll delight and surprise your palate when you use them to make icy sorbets, whether you choose banana, mango, or the less familiar passion fruit or cherimoya. For a real tropical treat, make three sorbets of different colors and layer them in a parfait glass.

½ **cup** *each* **sugar and water**
1 **cup fruit purée (choices and directions follow)**

In a 1- to 2-quart pan, stir together sugar and water. Bring to a boil over high heat; continue to boil, uncovered, until syrup is reduced to ½ cup (about 5 minutes). Let cool. If made ahead, cover and refrigerate (syrup will keep indefinitely).

Prepare fruit purée of your choice; mix syrup and purée. If desired, pour through a wire strainer to remove any seeds; discard residue. Pour mixture into an 8- or 9-inch square metal pan or a 5- by 9-inch metal loaf pan. Cover and freeze just until almost firm (about 1½ hours). Break fruit mixture into small chunks with a heavy spoon; turn into small bowl of an electric mixer and beat until slushy, increasing mixer speed from low to high as ice softens. Cover airtight and freeze until firm (about 2 hours). For best flavor and texture, serve sorbet within 1 month.

To serve hard-frozen sorbet, let stand at room temperature until slightly softened before scooping. Makes 3 servings (about 1½ cups *total*).

NOTE: If desired, you may freeze sorbet in a self-refrigerated ice cream maker according to manufacturer's directions. Serve when frozen soft, or store as directed for sorbet made in the freezer.

Fruit purée. All purées are most easily prepared by whirling fruit in a blender or food processor. You may also put fruit through a food mill or (for soft fruits) press it through a wire strainer.

Mango. Whirl 1 cup peeled, seeded, cubed **mango** (about 1 medium-size fruit) with 2½ tablespoons **orange juice** until smoothly puréed.

Babaco. Whirl 1¼ cups peeled, seeded, and coarsely chopped **babaco** (about 1 fruit) with 1½ teaspoons **lemon juice** until smoothly puréed.

Banana. Whirl 1¼ cups cubed **bananas** (about 3) with 1½ tablespoons **lemon juice** until smoothly puréed.

Cherimoya. Whirl 1¼ cups peeled, seeded, chopped **cherimoya** (about 1 medium-size fruit) with 2 tablespoons **orange juice** until smoothly puréed.

Feijoa. Whirl 1 cup **feijoa** pulp (scooped from 9 or 10 feijoas) with 1½ tablespoons **lemon juice** until smoothly puréed.

Guava. Whirl 1 cup **guava** pulp (scooped from 8 to 10 guavas) with 1½ tablespoons **lemon juice** until smoothly puréed.

Kiwi fruit. Whirl 1¼ cups peeled, sliced **kiwi fruit** (4 or 5 fruits) until smoothly puréed.

Papaya. Whirl 1 cup peeled, seeded, cubed **papaya** (about a 1-lb. fruit) with 2½ tablespoons **lime juice** until smoothly puréed.

Passion fruit. Whirl 1 cup **passion fruit** pulp (scooped from 8 to 12 passion fruits) until seeds are ground as fine as coarse pepper.

Pepino. Whirl 1 cup peeled, seeded **pepinos** (3 or 4 fruits) with 1 tablespoon **lemon juice** until smoothly puréed.

Sapote. Whirl 1 cup seeded **sapote** chunks (from 1 large peeled sapote) with 2 tablespoons **lemon juice** until smoothly puréed.

Tamarillo. Whirl 1 cup peeled, sliced **tamarillos** (4 or 5 fruits) with 1 tablespoon **lemon juice** until smoothly puréed.

Per serving of Mango Sorbet: .43 gram protein, 46 grams carbohydrates, .18 gram total fat, 0 milligram cholesterol, 2 milligrams sodium.

Coffee Snow

Preparation time: 40 to 50 minutes
Freezing time: at least 4 hours

Calories per serving: 74

Coffee lovers will appreciate this flavorful frozen dessert. To make it, you start with strong coffee, sweeten it with sugar and add a little coffee liqueur, then simply freeze the liquid in ice cube trays. Before serving, just whirl it to a slush in a food processor, then spoon into dessert dishes—or freeze it again until it's firm enough to scoop.

If you like, you can add milk to the coffee as directed below to make a refreshing treat we call frozen cappuccino.

- ½ **cup ground coffee**
- 4⅔ **cups water**
- ½ **cup sugar**
- ¼ **cup coffee-flavored liqueur (optional)**
  About ½ cup whipping cream
  Ground nutmeg or unsweetened cocoa

Prepare coffee by your favorite method, using ½ cup ground coffee and 4⅔ cups water. You should have 4 cups hot coffee. Stir sugar into coffee until dissolved; let cool. Stir in liqueur, if desired.

Pour coffee mixture into 2 or 3 divided ice cube trays. Cover and freeze until solid (at least 4 hours). Remove cubes from trays; use at once or transfer to plastic bags and store in freezer for up to 1 week.

Let cubes stand at room temperature for 10 to 15 minutes. Then whirl in a food processor, a portion at a time; use on-off pulses at first to break up cubes, then whirl continuously until smooth and slushy. (Or place all cubes in large bowl of an electric mixer; beat until smooth and slushy, increasing mixer speed from low to high as ice softens.) Serve dessert as a slush, or cover airtight and freeze until firm enough to scoop.

To serve, beat cream until it holds soft peaks; top each serving of coffee snow with cream and nutmeg. Makes 10 servings (about 5 cups *total*).

Per serving: .25 gram protein, 10 grams carbohydrates, 4 grams total fat, 13 milligrams cholesterol, 5 milligrams sodium.

Frozen Cappuccino

Follow directions for **Coffee Snow,** but prepare hot coffee with only 2 cups water. Stir sugar into hot coffee as directed; then stir in 2 cups **whole milk** and liqueur, if desired. Freeze, beat, and serve as directed for **Coffee Snow.**

Watermelon Snow

Preparation time: 50 to 60 minutes
Freezing time: about 6 hours total

Calories per serving: 83

If summer had a flavor, perhaps it would taste like this rum-spiked watermelon ice. Serve scoops of the ice to top off a barbecue, with wedges of lime to squeeze over each portion. Your guests will love it, and you'll appreciate the way it fits the casual nature of summer entertaining—you can make it long in advance and avoid any fuss at party time.

- ½ **cup sugar**
- 1 **cup water**
- 5 **to 6 pounds watermelon**
- ¼ **cup light or dark rum**
- ¼ **cup lime juice**
  Mint sprigs
  Lime wedges

In a 1- to 2-quart pan, combine sugar and water. Bring to a boil over high heat; then continue to boil, uncovered, stirring occasionally, until reduced to ½ cup. Let cool.

Cut off and discard watermelon rind. Cut fruit into chunks; pick out and discard seeds. Whirl melon, a portion at a time, in a blender or food processor until puréed. Rub purée through a fine wire strainer into a large bowl; discard any residue. You should have about 6 cups purée.

Stir sugar syrup, rum, and lime juice into watermelon purée. Pour into an 8- or 9-inch square metal pan, cover, and freeze until solid (3 to 4 hours).

Let ice stand at room temperature until you can break it into chunks with a heavy spoon. Place chunks in large bowl of an electric mixer; beat until smooth and slushy, increasing mixer speed from low to high as ice softens. (Or whirl chunks, a portion at a time, in a food processor; use on-off pulses at first to break up chunks, then whirl continuously until smooth and slushy.)

Return ice to metal pan, cover airtight, and freeze until firm (at least 3 hours). For best flavor and texture, serve ice within 3 months.

Let ice stand at room temperature until slightly softened (about 15 minutes) before scooping. Serve in bowls or stemmed glasses; garnish with mint. Offer lime wedges to squeeze over each portion. Makes 12 servings (about 1½ quarts *total*).

Per serving: .74 gram protein, 17 grams carbohydrates, .51 gram total fat, 0 milligram cholesterol, 3 milligrams sodium.

Gather 'round the ice cream maker and get ready for a light, lean, and delicious summer
dessert. It's Frozen Yogurt (recipe on page 72), brimming with
good-for-you ingredients. Choose vanilla or any of four fruit flavors.

• •

Blueberry Ice

Preparation time: 35 to 45 minutes
Freezing time: about 5 hours total

Calories per serving: 168

Summer's harvest of fresh blueberries is put to good use in this frosty blue dessert. A dash of cinnamon enhances the berries' distinctive flavor.

When shopping for fresh blueberries, choose firm, plump, dark blue berries with a light grayish bloom. Avoid cartons with stained bottoms—these probably contain overripe or moldy berries. Refrigerate fresh berries, unwashed, for up to 2 weeks.

    4 cups blueberries
    1¼ cups *each* sugar and water
    3 tablespoons lemon juice
       Dash *each* of salt and ground cinnamon
    3 egg whites

Cover and refrigerate 1 cup of the blueberries. Whirl remaining 3 cups blueberries in a blender or food processor until smoothly puréed. Add sugar, water, lemon juice, salt, and cinnamon; whirl until blended. Pour into an 8- or 9-inch square metal pan and freeze, uncovered, until solid (2 to 3 hours).

Let ice stand at room temperature until you can break it into chunks with a heavy spoon. Meanwhile, in small bowl of an electric mixer, beat egg whites until they hold soft, moist peaks.

Break up blueberry mixture and transfer to large bowl of mixer; beat until smooth and light-colored, increasing mixer speed from low to high as ice softens. Beat in about ¼ of the egg whites; gently fold in remaining egg whites. Cover ice airtight and freeze until firm (at least 3 hours) or until ready to serve.

To serve hard-frozen ice, let stand at room temperature until slightly softened; then scoop into 8 bowls and garnish each serving with 2 tablespoons of the reserved blueberries. Makes 8 servings.

Per serving: 2 grams protein, 42 grams carbohydrates, .28 gram total fat, 0 milligram cholesterol, 41 milligrams sodium.

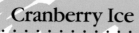

Cranberry Ice

Preparation time: 40 to 50 minutes
Freezing time: about 10 hours total

Calories per serving: 114

Many travelers to Mexico have discovered *paletas*—the fruit-flavored ices on sticks sold by street vendors and in fruit juice bars. Here's a selection of

velvety slushes inspired by *paletas* in the flavors of autumn; make the basic cranberry ice, or try persimmon or pomegranate. You might try serving these ices with holiday meals as a low-calorie dessert choice.

    4   cups (1 lb.) fresh or frozen cranberries
    1½ cups water
    ⅔   cup sugar (or to taste)
    ½   cup orange juice
    ½   teaspoon grated orange peel
    1   tablespoon lemon juice

In a 2-quart pan, combine cranberries and water. Cook, uncovered, over medium heat until skins pop; stir often. Pour berries and liquid into a wire strainer set over a large bowl. Press with the back of a spoon to force pulp through; discard residue. Add sugar, orange juice, orange peel, and lemon juice to cranberry pulp; stir until sugar is dissolved.

Pour cranberry mixture into an 8- or 9-inch square metal pan; cover and freeze until solid (at least 8 hours).

Let ice stand at room temperature until you can break it into chunks with a heavy spoon. Whirl chunks in a food processor, a portion at a time; use on-off pulses at first to break up chunks, then whirl continuously until mixture is smooth and slushy. (Or place all chunks in large bowl of an electric mixer; beat until smooth and slushy, increasing mixer speed from low to high as ice softens.)

Return ice to metal pan or pour into a metal bowl; cover airtight and freeze until firm (about 2 hours). For best flavor and texture, serve ice within 1 month. To serve hard-frozen ice, let stand at room temperature until slightly softened (about 10 minutes) before scooping. Makes 7 servings (about 3½ cups *total*).

Per serving: .37 gram protein, 29 grams carbohydrates, .13 gram total fat, 0 milligram cholesterol, 1 milligram sodium.

Persimmon Ice

Use very soft, ripe **Hachiya-type persimmons.** Cut 6 to 8 large persimmons in halves and scoop out flesh; discard skin, seeds, and stems. Whirl flesh in a food processor or blender until smooth; you should have 2 cups. Add 1 cup **water,** 3 tablespoons **lime juice,** 1 teaspoon grated **lime peel,** and ½ cup **sugar** (or to taste). Stir until sugar is dissolved. Freeze, beat, and serve as directed for **Cranberry Ice.** Garnish servings with **lime slices.** Makes 8 servings (about 1 quart *total*).

Pomegranate Ice

Remove seeds from 8 to 10 large **pomegranates;** you'll need 8 cups. In a food processor or blender, whirl 1½ to 2 cups seeds at a time until smooth. Line a wire strainer with cheesecloth and set it over a large bowl; pour seeds and juice through strainer. Let drain, saving liquid and discarding residue; you need 4 cups juice. To juice, add 1½ teaspoons grated **lemon peel,** 3 to 4 tablespoons **lemon juice,** and ¾ cup **sugar** (or to taste). Stir until sugar is dissolved. Freeze, beat, and serve as directed for **Cranberry Ice.** Garnish servings with **orange segments,** if desired. Makes 10 servings (about 5 cups *total*).

Orange Ice

Preparation time: 25 to 35 minutes
Freezing time: about 6 hours total

Calories per serving: 192

Citrus peel steeped in a base of sugar and water gives this orange ice a deliciously fresh, natural flavor. For an appealing presentation, freeze the ice in hollowed-out orange shells, then serve it directly from the freezer, garnished with a few shreds of orange peel.

> 2 **tablespoons grated orange peel**
> 1¼ **cups sugar**
> 1 **cup water**
> 1½ **cups orange juice**
> 2 **tablespoons lemon juice**

In a medium-size bowl, combine orange peel, sugar, and water. Cover and let stand for at least 4 hours; stir occasionally.

Stir mixture to combine sugar and liquid; then pour through a wire strainer and discard orange peel. Add orange juice and lemon juice. Pour mixture into an 8- or 9-inch square metal pan, cover, and freeze until solid (about 4 hours).

Let ice stand at room temperature until you can break it into chunks with a heavy spoon. Whirl chunks in a food processor, a portion at a time; use on-off pulses at first to break up chunks, then whirl continuously until smooth and slushy. (Or place all chunks in large bowl of an electric mixer; beat until smooth and slushy, increasing mixer speed from low to high as ice softens.)

Pour ice into a freezer container, cover airtight, and freeze until firm (about 2 hours). For best flavor and texture, serve ice within 2 months. To serve hard-frozen ice, let stand at room temperature until slightly softened before scooping. Makes 6 servings (about 3 cups *total*).

Per serving: .47 gram protein, 49 grams carbohydrates, .04 gram total fat, 0 milligram cholesterol, 2 milligrams sodium.

Lemon Ice

Preparation time: 50 to 60 minutes
Freezing time: about 6 hours total

Calories per serving: 90

Lemon zest and juice give this ice its refreshing tang. For best flavor, be sure to use freshly squeezed lemon juice—ice made with reconstituted juice just doesn't taste as good.

> 1 **small lemon**
> **About ½ cup lemon juice**
> 1 **cup sugar**
> 4 **cups water**
> **Dash of salt**

Using a vegetable peeler or a sharp knife, cut peel (yellow part only) from lemon. Squeeze juice from lemon into a glass measure; add enough additional fresh lemon juice to make ⅔ cup total. Cover juice and set aside.

Cut lemon peel into ½-inch pieces; place in a food processor along with sugar and whirl until peel is finely chopped. Pour mixture into a 3-quart pan, add water and salt, and heat, stirring, just until sugar is dissolved. Let cool; stir in lemon juice. Pour mixture into an 8- or 9-inch square metal pan, cover, and freeze until solid (about 4 hours).

Let ice stand at room temperature until you can break it into chunks with a heavy spoon. Whirl chunks in a food processor, a portion at a time; use on-off pulses at first to break up chunks, then whirl continuously until smooth and slushy. (Or place all chunks in large bowl of an electric mixer; beat until smooth and slushy, increasing mixer speed from low to high as ice softens.)

Pour ice into a freezer container, cover airtight, and freeze until firm (about 2 hours). For best flavor and texture, serve ice within 2 months. To serve hard-frozen ice, let stand at room temperature until slightly softened before scooping. Makes 9 servings (about 4½ cups *total*).

Per serving: .06 gram protein, 24 grams carbohydrates, 0 gram total fat, 0 milligram cholesterol, 15 milligrams sodium.

Vivid colors and intense fruit flavors are what you'll enjoy with
Strawberry Ice and Pineapple Ice (recipes on facing page).
These European-style fruit ices make an excellent finish to hot-weather meals.

. . . .

Strawberry Ice

(Pictured on facing page)
Preparation time: 30 to 40 minutes
Freezing time: about 7 hours total

Calories per serving: 96

This make-ahead dessert is full of fresh fruit flavor. Use strawberries in season, or try the pineapple or papaya variations. For a fancy European touch, garnish scoops of ice with flaky French fan wafers.

    4 cups hulled strawberries
    ½ cup *each* sugar and water
    2 tablespoons lemon juice
       Fan wafers (gaufrettes), orange slices, or
       shredded orange peel (optional)

In a food processor, whirl strawberries until puréed. Add sugar, water, and lemon juice; whirl until combined. Pour purée into divided ice cube trays, cover, and freeze until solid (at least 3 hours). Remove cubes from trays; use at once or transfer to plastic bags and store in freezer for up to 2 weeks.

To prepare ice, whirl cubes, a portion at a time, in a food processor; use on-off pulses at first to break up cubes, then whirl continuously until mixture is smooth and slushy. (Or place all cubes in large bowl of an electric mixer; beat until smooth and slushy, increasing mixer speed from low to high as ice softens.) Pour mixture into an 8- or 9-inch square metal pan, cover airtight, and freeze until solid (at least 4 hours) or for up to 1 week.

To serve, let ice stand at room temperature until you can break it into chunks with a heavy spoon. Whirl in a food processor until smooth and free of ice crystals. Serve at once, garnished with fan wafers, if desired. Makes 6 servings (about 3 cups *total*).

Per serving: .63 gram protein, 24 grams carbohydrates, .38 gram total fat, 0 milligram cholesterol, 2 milligrams sodium.

Pineapple Ice
(Pictured on facing page)

Peel and core 1 large **pineapple;** cut into chunks. Whirl in a food processor, a portion at a time, until puréed (you should have 4 cups purée). Stir in 1 cup **water,** 2 tablespoons **sugar** (or to taste), and 2 tablespoons **lemon juice.** Freeze, beat, and serve as directed for **Strawberry Ice.** Garnish with small slices of **fresh pineapple,** if desired. Makes 10 servings (about 5 cups *total*).

Papaya Ice

Peel, halve, and seed 1 large **papaya;** cut into chunks. Whirl in a food processor until puréed; you should have 1¼ cups. Stir in 2 tablespoons **lime juice,** 3 tablespoons **sugar,** and ⅓ cup **water.** Freeze, beat, and serve as directed for **Strawberry Ice.** Makes 3 servings (about 1⅔ cups *total*).

Cabernet Sauvignon Ice

Preparation time: about 30 minutes
Chilling time: about 1 hour
Freezing time: about 6 hours total

Calories per serving: 108

Garnished with mint sprigs and red grapes, this cool and frosty ice makes a sophisticated dessert. If you like, you can also serve it in small portions alongside grilled meat, or as a palate-refresher between courses.

    ¾   cup sugar
    1   cup water
    1½ cups Cabernet Sauvignon
    1½ cups white grape juice
    ¾   cup lemon juice
        Mint sprigs (optional)
        Red grapes (optional)

In a 1- to 1½-quart pan, combine sugar, water, and wine. Bring to a boil; then reduce heat and simmer gently, uncovered, for 5 minutes. Let cool. Stir in grape juice and lemon juice; cover and refrigerate until cold (at least 1 hour).

Pour mixture into 2 or 3 divided ice cube trays or an 8- or 9-inch square metal pan. Cover and freeze until solid (about 4 hours). If ice has been frozen in a pan, let stand at room temperature until you can break it into chunks with a heavy spoon.

Whirl frozen cubes or chunks, a portion at a time, in a food processor; use on-off pulses at first to break up ice, then whirl continuously until smooth and slushy. (Or place all cubes or chunks in large bowl of an electric mixer and beat until smooth and slushy, increasing mixer speed from low to high as ice softens.)

Pour ice into a freezer container, cover airtight, and freeze until firm (about 2 hours). For best flavor and texture, serve within 1 month.

To serve hard-frozen ice, let stand at room temperature until slightly softened before scooping. Garnish each serving with mint sprigs and grapes, if desired. Makes 8 servings (about 5 cups *total*).

Per serving: .21 gram protein, 28 grams carbohydrates, .10 gram total fat, 0 milligram cholesterol, 8 milligrams sodium.

Dessert Drinks
SWEETS FOR SIPPING

Imagine sitting before a crackling fire on a snowy night, a mug of something warm and sweet in your hand. Or perhaps strolling through a summer garden party, nibbling ladyfingers and sipping a tall glass of sparkling punch.

Need we say more? Dessert beverages lend an inviting, festive touch to your meals, turning the simplest fare into something special. Some of the following dessert drinks are hot, some cold; some are made with alcohol, some without. Most would be delightful with fresh fruit or a couple of cookies served alongside, but the richest ones—Mexican Hot Chocolate, for example—stand alone as desserts in themselves.

Pastel Fruit Slush

Preparation time: 20 to 30 minutes (does not include freezing time)

Calories per serving of Peach Slush: 209

Frozen cubed fruit blended with buttermilk, milk, or yogurt makes a smooth, cooling beverage that's both delicious and wholesome. Instead of diluting the drink as ice would, the fruit imparts a full, tangy flavor and a thick, slushy texture.

Choose peach, strawberry, pineapple, or watermelon slush; if you wish, serve each drink with a few Won Ton Cinnamon Crisps (page 20).

> 1½ **cups frozen fruit cubes (choices and directions follow)**
> ⅓ **cup buttermilk, lowfat milk, or plain lowfat yogurt**
> 2 **to 4 teaspoons sugar**
> **Mint sprigs (optional)**

Cube and freeze fruit of your choice as directed.

To prepare slush, let frozen fruit stand at room temperature until slightly softened (about 5 minutes). Pour buttermilk into a blender or food processor. With motor running, add a few fruit cubes at a time (keep top of blender covered to prevent splashing); whirl until mixture is slushy. Blend in sugar.

Pour slush into a glass; top with mint, if desired. Serve at once. Makes 1 serving.

Frozen fruit cubes. Choose 1 of the following.

Peach cubes. Peel and pit **peaches.** Cut into about ¾-inch chunks. Dip in **lemon juice** to coat, then set slightly apart in a single layer in a shallow pan. Cover and freeze until solid. With a wide spatula, slide fruit from pan into plastic bags or freezer containers; store in freezer until ready to use.

Strawberry cubes. Cut hulled **strawberries** into about ¾-inch chunks. Freeze as directed for **peach cubes** (do not dip in lemon juice before freezing).

Pineapple cubes. Cut off top and base of **pineapple,** then slice off peel deep enough to remove eyes. Cut out and remove core. Cut fruit into about ¾-inch chunks. Freeze as directed for **peach cubes** (do not dip in lemon juice before freezing).

Watermelon cubes. Cut **watermelon** into ¾-inch-thick slices. Cut off and discard rind. Cut fruit into ¾-inch cubes. Remove and discard seeds. Freeze as directed for **peach cubes** (do not dip in lemon juice before freezing).

Per serving of Peach Slush: 5 grams protein, 50 grams carbohydrates, 1 gram total fat, 3 milligrams cholesterol, 88 milligrams sodium.

Spiced Lemonade

Preparation time: 30 to 45 minutes

Calories per serving of Spiced Lemonade made with Mint Syrup: 109

Rediscover lemonade with this intriguing recipe— you sweeten the classic summer beverage with tangy flavored syrups. Choose mint, ginger, or cardamom syrup, or offer all three and let your guests take their pick.

One has the refreshing taste of mint, another the spicy-sweet flavor of fresh ginger, and the third the aromatic appeal of cardamom. To allow guests to flavor their own beverages to taste, offer one, two, or all three syrups with the lemonade; let each guest mix his or her own serving.

> **Spiced Syrup (recipes follow)**
> 6 **cups water**
> 1½ **cups lemon juice**
> **Ice cubes**
> **Thin lemon slices**

Prepare syrup of your choice; let cool.

In a 2- to 3-quart pitcher, mix water and lemon juice. Pour into ice-filled glasses. Add syrup to each glass to taste, allowing 1½ to 2½ tablespoons for each 1 cup of lemonade. Garnish with lemon slices. Makes about 8 servings.

Spiced Syrup. Use any of the following 3 flavors. If stored in the refrigerator, syrups keep for up to 2 months.

Mint Syrup. In a 3- to 4-quart pan, combine 2 cups coarsely chopped **fresh mint** (leaves and stems); 1 cup **sugar;** 4 cups **water;** and 3 strips **lemon peel** (*each* ½ by 2 inches, yellow part only). Bring to a boil over high heat; continue to boil, uncovered, until liquid is reduced to 1 cup (to measure, pour syrup through a wire strainer set over a glass measure). Discard mint; let syrup cool.

Ginger Syrup. In a 1½- to 2-quart pan, combine 1 cup (5 oz.) peeled, coarsely chopped **fresh ginger;** 1 cup **sugar;** 3 cups **water;** and 3 strips **lemon peel** (*each* ½ by 2 inches, yellow part only). Bring to a boil over high heat; continue to boil, uncovered, until liquid is reduced to 1 cup (to measure, pour syrup through a wire strainer set over a glass measure). Discard ginger; let syrup cool.

Cardamom Syrup. Follow directions for **Ginger Syrup,** but omit ginger and use 40 **cardamom pods,** cracked open. Discard pods after cooking.

Per serving of Spiced Lemonade made with Mint Syrup: .34 gram protein, 28 grams carbohydrates, .20 gram total fat, 0 milligram cholesterol, 10 milligrams sodium.

Tangerine-Peach Fizz

(Pictured on facing page)
Preparation time: 20 to 30 minutes

Calories per serving: 95

Festive and fruity, this effervescent punch is a good choice for a party. You can make it with either sparkling wine or sparkling water, depending on the occasion and your own preference. When you serve the punch, be sure to provide spoons for eating the blueberries and peaches.

> **4 ripe peaches (about 1 lb. *total*), peeled**
> **1 tablespoon lemon juice**
> **1 can (6 oz.) frozen unsweetened tangerine juice concentrate, partially thawed**
> **½ to 1 teaspoon ground cinnamon**
> **½ cup blueberries**
> **1 bottle (about 750 ml.) sparkling muscat wine or 3 cups sparkling water, chilled**
> **Lime slices (optional)**

Pit and thinly slice 2 of the peaches. Put into a small bowl and mix with lemon juice to coat; set aside.

Pit remaining 2 peaches and cut into chunks; place in a blender or food processor and add tangerine juice concentrate and cinnamon. Whirl until smooth. Pour into a 2½- to 3-quart punch bowl. Gently stir in sliced peaches, blueberries, and wine. Ladle into glasses; garnish with lime slices, if desired. Sip punch; eat fruit with a spoon. Makes 12 servings.

Per serving: .55 gram protein, 14 grams carbohydrates, .10 gram total fat, 0 milligram cholesterol, 4 milligrams sodium.

Citrus Spritzer

Preparation time: 15 to 20 minutes

Calories per serving: 70

Garnished with a lime slice, a tall glass of this bubbly drink is showy enough for a party—and simple enough to make for an afternoon refresher. Try it with a slice of angel food cake and a few strawberries, for a dessert that tastes like a splurge but has fewer than 225 calories.

> **4 or 5 large oranges**
> **2 or 3 large limes**
> **1 bottle (24 oz.) or 3 cups white grape juice**
> **Ice cubes**
> **About 3 cups sparkling water, chilled**

With a vegetable peeler, cut strips of citrus peel (*each* ½ by 3 inches, colored part only): 3 strips from

1 orange, 2 strips from 1 lime. Place peel in a pitcher; bruise with a wooden spoon.

Squeeze oranges to make 2 cups juice. Cut 5 thin center slices from 1 lime; cut each slice in half and set aside. (If making more than 4 hours ahead, reserve 1 whole lime; cut slices just before serving.) Squeeze remaining limes to make ¼ cup juice. Add orange juice, lime juice, and grape juice to pitcher; mix. Serve at once; or cover and refrigerate for up to 24 hours.

For each serving, fill a glass with ice and about 2 parts juice to 1 part sparkling water. Garnish drinks with halved lime slices. Makes 10 servings.

Per serving: .78 gram protein, 17 grams carbohydrates, .15 gram total fat, 0 milligram cholesterol, 3 milligrams sodium.

Double Raspberry Cooler

Preparation time: 5 to 10 minutes

Calories per serving: 101

Raspberries appear in two forms in this cold dessert drink. The beverage is based on black raspberry liqueur and sparkling water; fresh raspberries add a special touch.

For an equally refreshing cooler, try our tropical variation, made with guava juice or nectar and flavored with orange and lime.

> **3 cups cracked ice**
> **1½ cups raspberries**
> **12 thin lemon slices**
> **¾ cup black raspberry liqueur or raspberry syrup**
> **About 3 cups sparkling water, chilled**

Divide ice, raspberries, and lemon slices equally among six 8-ounce glasses. Pour 2 tablespoons of the liqueur into each glass. Fill with sparkling water; serve with spoons so you can muddle the fruit. Makes 6 servings.

Per serving: .48 gram protein, 14 grams carbohydrates, .21 gram total fat, 0 milligram cholesterol, .54 milligram sodium.

Tropical Cooler

Follow directions for **Double Raspberry Cooler,** but substitute 12 **lime slices** for the lemon slices. Omit black raspberry liqueur. Instead, use a mixture of 3 cups **guava juice** or guava nectar and 6 tablespoons **orange-flavored liqueur;** reduce sparkling water to 1½ cups.

Summer's sweet harvest of peaches and blueberries is put to good use in
Tangerine-Peach Fizz (recipe on facing page).
Sip the sparkling punch from a glass, then eat the fruit with a spoon.

· ·

Coffee & Cream Frappé

Preparation time: 5 to 10 minutes

Calories per serving: 39

Lemon juice gives an unexpected accent to this foamy cold drink. It's an icy and refreshing treat for summertime enjoyment.

- 3 tablespoons lemon juice
- 2 tablespoons *each* powdered sugar and whipping cream
- 2 teaspoons instant coffee
- 2 cups cracked ice
- 1 cup ginger ale

In a blender, whirl lemon juice, sugar, cream, and coffee until foamy. Add ice and whirl until smooth, using several on-off pulses. Add ginger ale and whirl on low speed just until blended. Makes 6 servings.

Per serving: .13 gram protein, 6 grams carbohydrates, 2 grams total fat, 6 milligrams cholesterol, 4 milligrams sodium.

Café au Chocolat Blanc

Preparation time: 10 to 15 minutes

Calories per serving: 151

Here's a hot dessert or breakfast drink that's a cross between hot chocolate and French *café au lait.* To make it, you combine strong coffee with a steaming blend of hot milk and white chocolate. (To prepare for children, omit the coffee and stir ground sweet chocolate to taste into the hot white chocolate.)

- 4 cups hot, strong coffee (directions follow)
- 4 cups lowfat milk
- 4 ounces white chocolate or white pastel coating, chopped
- 2 tablespoons sugar

Prepare coffee. Meanwhile, in a 2- to 3-quart pan, combine milk, white chocolate, and sugar. Stir frequently over medium heat until chocolate is melted and milk is steaming. If made ahead, let cool; then cover and refrigerate for up to 2 days. Reheat before using.

To serve, pour about ½ cup *each* steaming hot chocolate and hot coffee into cups. Makes 8 servings.

Strong coffee. Brew coffee using double the amount of **ground coffee** that you'd normally use.

Per serving: 5 grams protein, 18 grams carbohydrates, 7 grams total fat, 12 milligrams cholesterol, 74 milligrams sodium.

Blender Cappuccino

Preparation time: 10 to 15 minutes

Calories per serving: 47

The Italian specialty known as cappuccino is often enjoyed at coffeehouses and restaurants that have espresso machines. This version can be made at home, without any special equipment other than a blender. Topped with frothy spoonfuls of milk foam and dusted with cocoa, the cups of hot, strong coffee make an elegant ending for a meal, alone or with a light dessert.

- 3 to 4 cups hot, strong coffee (directions at left, below)
- 3 cups lowfat milk
  Sugar
  Unsweetened cocoa

Prepare coffee.

In a 1- to 1½-quart pan, scald milk over medium-low heat. Pour milk into a blender; cover (hold lid on tightly with a thick towel) and whirl until frothy. Pour milk and coffee into separate pitchers. Place sugar and cocoa on the table in separate containers.

To serve, pour about ½ cup *each* hot coffee and milk into a cup, then spoon some of the milk foam on top. Sprinkle cappuccino lightly with cocoa and sweeten to taste with sugar. Makes 6 to 8 servings.

Per serving: 3 grams protein, 4 grams carbohydrates, 2 grams total fat, 7 milligrams cholesterol, 47 milligrams sodium.

Mexican Hot Chocolate

(Pictured on page 94)
Preparation time: 15 to 20 minutes

Calories per serving: 291

When you simply *must* have something chocolaty, try serving this warm, sweet beverage for dessert. Made with almonds, cinnamon, and bittersweet chocolate, it's authentically Mexican in flavor but modern in method: to whip it to a froth, you use a blender instead of the traditional carved wooden *molinillo.* We suggest garnishing each serving with a 3-inch cinnamon stick, but if you like, use long cinnamon stick "stirrers."

- 4 cups lowfat milk
- 6 cinnamon sticks (*each* about 3 inches long)
- 6 ounces bittersweet or semisweet chocolate, broken into pieces
- ⅓ cup slivered almonds
- 2 tablespoons sugar

In a 1½- to 2-quart pan, combine milk and 3 of the cinnamon sticks. Warm over low heat; stir occasionally. Meanwhile, place chocolate, almonds, and sugar in a blender; whirl until a coarse powder forms. If desired, remove a little of the chocolate powder from blender and reserve for garnish.

Increase heat under milk to high and stir milk until it is just at the boiling point. Lift out cinnamon sticks; rinse, dry, and set aside for garnish. Pour 2 cups of the hot milk into blender; cover (hold lid on tightly with a thick towel) and whirl until blended. Add remaining 2 cups milk and whirl, covered, until blended. Place 1 cinnamon stick in each of 6 mugs; fill mugs with hot, foamy chocolate. If desired, sprinkle each serving with some of the reserved chocolate powder. Makes 6 servings.

Per serving: 8 grams protein, 31 grams carbohydrates, 17 grams total fat, 13 milligrams cholesterol, 83 milligrams sodium.

Quick Swedish Glögg

Preparation time: 20 to 25 minutes

Calories per serving: 196

At Christmastime in Sweden, the traditional beverage is a hot mulled wine known as *glögg*. To prepare for a holiday gathering, a Swedish family might steep spices in wine for several hours or even days. Our recipe gives you the flavor and comforting warmth of glögg, but takes much less time to prepare.

  1 cup *each* water and dry red wine
  3 tablespoons sugar
  2 cardamom pods, cracked open
  ½ teaspoon whole cloves
  1 cinnamon stick (about 3 inches long)
1½ tablespoons raisins

In a small pan, combine water, wine, sugar, cardamom, cloves, and cinnamon stick. Bring to a boil over high heat; then reduce heat and simmer, uncovered, for 8 minutes.

Pour wine mixture through a wire strainer; discard spices. Pour wine mixture back into pan, add raisins, and simmer, uncovered, for 2 more minutes.

Meanwhile, preheat 2 heavy glasses or mugs by filling them to the brim with very hot water. To serve, empty glasses and fill with hot spiced wine; spoon in raisins. Makes 2 servings.

Per serving: .40 gram protein, 30 grams carbohydrates, .16 gram total fat, 0 milligram cholesterol, 8 milligrams sodium.

Buttered Hot Cider

Preparation time: 20 to 25 minutes

Calories per serving: 268

Spiced apple cider laced with dark rum makes a good chill-chaser on a winter's evening. For a touch of richness, float a pat of butter atop each serving.

  2 cups apple cider
  ½ teaspoon whole cloves
  2 cinnamon sticks (*each* about 3 inches long)
  ⅛ teaspoon ground nutmeg
  2 teaspoons sugar
  ⅓ cup dark rum or apple cider
  2 pats (1 teaspoon *each*) butter or margarine

In a small pan, combine the 2 cups cider, cloves, cinnamon sticks, nutmeg, and sugar. Bring to a boil over high heat; then reduce heat and simmer gently, uncovered, for 10 minutes. Stir in rum; pour mixture through a wire strainer and discard spices.

Preheat 2 heavy glasses or mugs by filling them to the brim with very hot water. Empty glasses and fill with hot cider. Top each serving with 1 pat of the butter. Makes 2 servings.

Per serving: .29 gram protein, 35 grams carbohydrates, 4 grams total fat, 10 milligrams cholesterol, 49 milligrams sodium.

Chaudeau

Preparation time: 5 to 10 minutes

Calories per serving: 68

Chaudeau, a traditional European dessert, is a hot froth of eggs, wine, and sugar that's served in wine glasses for sipping. Be sure to serve it right away—its heavenly foaminess doesn't last.

  2 eggs
  ¼ cup sugar
  1 cup fruity white wine (such as Gewürztraminer, Chenin Blanc, or Johannisberg Riesling)

In a 2½- to 3-quart pan, combine eggs, sugar, and wine. Set over high heat and beat constantly with a portable electric mixer until mixture is foamy and has increased 3 to 4 times in volume (about 5 minutes).

Remove from heat, pour into wine glasses, and serve immediately. Makes 6 to 8 servings.

Per serving: 2 grams protein, 8 grams carbohydrates, 1 gram total fat, 68 milligrams cholesterol, 19 milligrams sodium.

Delicately flavored with cinnamon and almonds and whipped to a velvety froth,
steaming Mexican Hot Chocolate (recipe on page 92)
offers a nice change of pace from the standard cup of cocoa.

· ·